THE
ENGAGED
WOMAN'S
SURVIVAL
GUIDE

THE ENGAGED WOMAN'S SURVIVAL GUIDE

ARLENE MODICA MATTHEWS

FAWCETT COLUMBINE · NEW YORK

For Piper, Yvette, and Zoe

A Fawcett Columbine Book
Published by Ballantine Books
Copyright © 1993 by Arlene Modica Matthews

All rights reserved under International and
Pan-American Copyright Conventions. Published in the
United States by Ballantine Books, a division of Random House, Inc.,
New York, and simultaneously in Canada by Random
House of Canada Limited, Toronto.

Library of Congress Catalog Card Number: 92-73733

ISBN: 0-449-90756-2

Cover design by Dale Fiorillo

Text design by Holly Johnson

Manufactured in the United States of America

First Edition: January 1993

10 9 8 7 6 5 4 3 2 1

CONTENTS

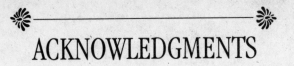

ACKNOWLEDGMENTS

My thanks to Julie Merberg, who edited this book, and to Carla Glasser, my agent. Most of all, I am indebted to the many women who shared with me what they experienced and what they felt during the months leading up to their weddings.

THE
ENGAGED
WOMAN'S
SURVIVAL
GUIDE

DO YOU HAVE PRE-MARITAL SYNDROME?

So, you're engaged to be married. Congratulations are in order. Doubtless you've received best wishes from practically everyone you've ever met.

People say they're thrilled for you, and, come to think of it, you *do* recall that trampolining-on-the-clouds sensation you felt not long ago—and still feel at times.

But now perhaps you have other feelings and fixations as well.

Perhaps, for example, you are concerned about how your engagement is affecting your other relationships:

Are you trying—and failing—to plan a wedding to please everyone in your family and everyone in his?

Is your mother making you cry, or vice versa, at least once a week?

Is Mom serious about your Cousin Wayne singing "Feelings" at your reception?

Is your best friend's envy making her a tad hostile?

Is your future sister-in-law annoyingly chummy?

Perhaps, too, you are wondering if the state of wedlock will wipe out your independence and individuality:

Is there really going to be enough room for your Pueblo pottery collection in your fiancé's apartment?

Why is he complaining all of a sudden when you have to work on the weekend?

Will changing your surname cause your credit history to vaporize in some computer bank?

Perhaps you are wondering if saying yes was such a good idea in the first place:

Are you and your man so preoccupied with wedding details that you don't speak of much else anymore?

Are you fighting over money?

Is your sex life in neutral?

Have his table manners been gradually vanishing since he placed that ring on your finger?

Do you worry that marriage may kill any vestige of romance in your relationship?

Do you wonder about the boyfriends you left behind, or the thousands of potential mates you haven't even met yet?

Does your father lament, "You could have done better?"

Do you sometimes think he's right?

If you've answered yes to three or more of these questions, you are experiencing a bona fide case of Pre-Marital Syndrome. Its primary symptoms are anxiety, irritability, guilt, tears, and trepidation—about the impending nuptials themselves, about the impact of your wedding on your family and friends, about how marriage will change you, and most of all, about the wisdom of sanctifying a romantic relationship that suddenly seems so fraught with misunderstandings.

Fear not. Pre-Marital Syndrome is experienced by the vast majority of brides-to-be. As a psychotherapist and couples' counselor, I have run across it innumerable times. Most women—and most relationships—survive it.

But perhaps you would like to do more than just survive. That's good, because you *can* flourish and thrive during the time of your engagement. But to do so, you need to face up to your particular assortment of doubts and dreads and see what you can learn.

This book is meant to help you do just that. It's a "bridal guide" of a different sort. Rather than focusing on the phrasing of your invitations or the selection of your silverware pattern, it offers anecdotes to assure you you are not alone, and advice to see you through some of your knottier Pre-Marital Syndrome problems—from family trials to financial tribulations to second thoughts and "cold feet." It also contains a liberal dose of humor—one of the best Pre-Marital Syndrome remedies ever discovered.

Using these emotional instruments, the book will teach you how to:

• Define your expectations and discern those of your future spouse
• Develop practical skills and strategies that will help you enhance not only the months of engagement but the years of postnuptial togetherness that loom ahead
• Break bad communication habits—with your spouse, his family and your own—before they get set in stone
• Dispel some of your fears and frustrations—about your wedding, about marriage in general, and about your man in particular—by unearthing the fallacies that may underlie those fears

You can use your engagement period to become a keen observer of the dynamics that are even now molding your marital relationship. And you can employ your newfound awareness to become an effective shaper of your own future. This is a serious goal. However, this book is meant to be not only useful, but fun. It is meant to be enjoyed, just as one's engagement months are a time to be enjoyed, once Pre-Marital Syndrome is under control.

CHAPTER ONE

A MOMENT OF ENGAGEMENT

This is it. You're in an elegant restaurant, seated across from the man whose proposal you've been wishing for for months. You accept the tiny velvet box with the sparkling diamond inside and gaze into his eyes. And, yes, you accept his marriage proposal. Finally things are just as you've always wanted them to be. Aren't they?

Well, yes. But be honest. Isn't there a part of you that can't help but wonder: Will it be downhill from here? What will all those years of domesticity do to him? Will you wake up one day to find yourself sitting a bowl of bran flakes away from a guy with the spontaneity of Ward Cleaver, the generosity of Fred Mertz, and the physique of Fred Flintstone?

And what will marriage do to *you*? Are you going to take on the June, Ethel, or Wilma role to match your husband's new persona? Are you going to turn into a predictable drudge, like your married friends? Or—gasp!—are you going to turn into your *mother*?

Welcome to the sorority of engaged women everywhere. This little "spoiler" voice inside you is all part of the usual course of events that takes place once you've responded affirmatively to your boyfriend's "big question." It's a natural reaction to facing your transition from "girlfriend" to fiancée, and anticipating the label of "wife." The question is: What are you going to do about this little voice?

Will you stifle your flutters of apprehension and pretend that your expectations of marriage are solely rose-colored? Will you let the vague disquietude nibbling at your joy proceed to take over completely, turning you into a moody and raw-nerved prenuptial wreck? Or will you vacillate between these two attitudes, insisting "everything's perfect" one minute and "everything's awful" the next?

RIGHTEOUS ROMANTICS, TEARY TESTERS, AND HALFWAY HYSTERICS

In my years of working with women in the throes of what I call Pre-Marital Syndrome, I've noticed that its symptoms, if left unattended, usually result in one of these three emotional positions. The first type of prospective bride—let's call her the Righteous Romantic—deals with her unwanted doubts and dread by denying, to herself and to everyone else, that they even exist. She puts her true emotional life on hold for the entire term of her engagement, often getting disproportionately obsessed in orchestrating the minutiae of wedding-day details, which leaves her precious little time to think about anything else.

Should grievances toward her partner arise, the Righteous Romantic willfully defers dealing with them until after the wedding. Should she feel uneasy, she shelves that feeling. Should someone else notice she seems anxious, she protests, "I am not!" *Just get me to the church on time,* this woman insists, then I'll deal with reality.

Unlike the tightly controlled Righteous Romantic, some betrothed women have thoroughly tumultuous engagement periods. Let's call such a woman a Teary Tester, because she is wont both to cry a lot and to treat every issue, no matter how minor, that arises between herself and her fiancé as the ultimate test of their future marital success. Just as soon as her betrothal is a *fait accompli,* the Teary Tester zooms straight into emotional hyperspace and stays there for the months during which she is inexorably bound for the altar.

She finds, suddenly and surprisingly, that she disagrees with her spouse-to-be about everything from what color the reception placemats ought to be, to whether or not the two of them should open a joint checking account, to where they plan to retire when they're sixty-five. Occasionally, though, this bride-to-be takes a break from complaining to her long-suffering fiancé . . . so that she can complain *about* him to anyone who will listen, including her friends, his friends, her maid of honor, her caterer, her stationer, and her florist. Soon *everyone* is mopping up after the Teary Tester.

Lastly we have a third kind of fiancée. Let's call her the Halfway Hysteric. Although she is listed last, the majority of engaged women fall into this category of Pre-Marital Syndrome sufferers. You see, the Halfway Hysteric is a cross between the the Righteous Romantic and the Teary Tester. Her behavior fluctuates between the two modes, often shifting with meteoric speed.

At certain times times she's stalwart in her insistence that everything is peachy-keen-thank-you-very-much. Armed with her checklists and her fabric swatches, she's the five-star general of weddings. Nothing is going to rattle her, rile her, or slip through her vigilant fingers. But at other times she is easily reducible to a weeping heap of worries and woes. She sobs and sighs, whimpers and whines about the "insensitive brute" or "hopeless bore" with whom she's about to pledge to spend her life. But though she may routinely awaken her best friend in the middle of the night to lament her fate, the next morning she may well assert she's "fine-thank-you" once again as she merrily trips off to sample canapés and purchase a new Vuitton garment bag.

THE MARITAL MARATHON

You may well recognize yourself as one of these three types of brides-to-be. If so, do not despair. What all these ladies—and you—have in common is simple. Each and every one is trying, in her own way, to come to terms with a good old-fashioned case of nerves.

Now, no one can blame a bride-to-be for being a little edgy. The prospect of a lifetime with one man—*any* man— is daunting. And nowadays "a lifetime" means something quite different than it used to. Back when the institution of marriage first gained wide acceptance, humans had less than half the lifespan they do now, and the number of years one was ex- pected to spend with a spouse was about the same length of time we might today hang on to a Honda Civic. However, contemporary men and women who are marrying in their twenties, thirties, or even forties face the prospect of fifty or more years of wedlock. It's not just marriage you'll be facing, but a legal, social, emotional, sexual, and financial marathon *à deux* that can easily span half a century.

Suppose you are wrong? Suppose this is some awful, ill- fated blunder? The thought is enough to make any engaged woman quake with apprehension. Of course, you may remind yourself that your nuptial event is unlike marital unions in the Dark Ages, when brides were commonly abducted and wed by force—and when, incidentally, the "best man" and "ushers" were brawny mates of the groom whose purpose was to help him capture the woman he desired.

Today, marriage comes with an "escape clause." But let's face it: The thought of divorce is wildly disagreeable, not only because you genuinely love this fellow you're planning to wed, but because we are living in an era when the concepts of "commitment" and "family values" are enjoying a tremendous resurgence in popularity. We have gone from the "me" decade to the "we" decade. For reasons both romantic and idealistic, as well as practical and realistic, just about everyone wants to be part of a couple—a married couple. What's more, they want to stay that way.

Yet you must be aware—even if you'd prefer *not* to be at this early stage of your union—that to avoid becoming a divorce statistic may well require coping with and working through some very knotty problems in your relationship. It's no secret, nor is there any shame in the fact, that two separate individuals will sometimes disagree. And it's only natural to worry about things we have no way of predicting or controlling. If you *weren't* nervous, *then* something would be wrong.

ANXIETY OVERDRIVE

Anxiety is clearly an appropriate response to such a major life change and such an awesome responsibility.

But there's no need to let that anxiety get the best of you and carry you away, influencing your behavior in ways that don't do you, your man, or anyone else participating in your wedding experience much good. Instead, try to see what this case of nerves has to teach you about yourself and your relationship to others.

It may help to hear what some women who were catapulted into "anxiety overdrive" on the way to their wedding have to say about the path they took—the path, that is, that *you* want to avoid.

For example, Cyndi, who was a Righteous Romantic when she married at age twenty-eight, recalls:

I was single-mindedly focused on my wedding day. I was so intent on making everything perfect. I guess I had the feeling that it *had* to be perfect or it might not bode well for my marriage. I guess you could have called me obsessive. I must have interviewed a dozen videographers, for example, and I made my bridesmaid try on about a hundred gowns all over the city.

I started to neglect everything else in my life, including my job. At first my co-workers and boss tried to be understanding about my being out of the office so much, or being on the phone making wedding plans all the time. But finally their workload became unbearable because of all the things I wasn't doing. I got one warning, then another. I was so embarrassed, but I could *not* stop worrying about the wedding and ignoring everything else.

In the end I decided I simply had to take a leave of absence so that I could finish everything that needed to be finished before the "big day." Of course, this meant a big drop in income, which didn't thrill my boyfriend, since our wedding cost a fortune and we were shouldering a lot of the bills ourselves. But I insisted the wedding had to be flawless and that this was the only way it could be. In the end he had to put in extra hours doing free-lance work to help pay the wedding expenses.

As you can see, Cyndi's particular style of anxiety took both a financial toll and a toll on her relationship with her fiancé. This was rather ironic, of course. Cyndi was convinced that her wedding and her marriage should be nothing less than perfect, yet she set things off on the wrong foot by remaining oblivious to her partner's preferences and by virtually assuring that she and he had very little prewedding time for meaningful communication. How could they think or talk about the future with any clarity when she was too busy planning and he was too busy with extra work?

Elise, a Teary Tester who wed at age thirty, allowed anxiety to do another kind of damage as her wedding day approached:

I was really thrilled when my boyfriend proposed marriage, and I rushed to tell everyone the good news. Within twenty-four hours of our engagement I must have called all my old college friends all over the country. Then he and I had an argument. I don't remember what it was about, but I think it had something to do with his apartment, which was always a mess but which suddenly seemed to really bother me because, you know, we were *engaged* now and I thought, "Is he going to be this messy when we're *married*?" Well, before I knew it I was calling these old friends back saying, "Hey, maybe I was being hasty. I mean, why rush to get married? I'm still young."

Now, this first incident set the tone for the next six months—at which point we finally did get married. But we fought so much up until the wedding day—mostly because I thought my boyfriend was too set in his bachelor ways—that I seriously considered calling it off a dozen times. And each time it would have meant more people to disinvite to the wedding, more gifts to return, more explanations, more *disgrace*.

I became a basket case just thinking about it. My nerves were shot. I got insomnia. I lost my appetite— well, for anything but chocolate. And then my skin broke out. The week before the wedding, after yet another argument, I got a whopper of a cold, which I'm sure was from all my self-imposed stress. I strode down the aisle clutching tissues along with my bouquet, and I could barely say, "I do," for sneezing.

Clearly, Elise's brand of premarital frenzy taxed her physically as well as emotionally. She is probably right in surmising that her "self-imposed stress" was a prime factor in creating her severe cold. Almost certainly it engendered her insomnia and erratic appetite. As for her relationship, disharmony prevailed. Her anxious "testing" doubtless caused her man an elevated stress level of his very own.

Finally, here is how Margo, who was twenty-four years old during her era of Halfway Hysteria, recalls the effect of anxiety on her prenuptial state:

> I rode an emotional roller coaster for an entire year before my marriage. And I brought my whole family along for the ride. One minute I was happy, then tearful and terrified. My mood swings confused everyone. I remember one Sunday I went to dinner at my parents' house without my fiancé. I told my mother, father, and brother that I didn't think I could go through with this wedding, at least not now. They seemed horrified, and I got furious. What did they know about my life, anyway?
>
> The next night my parents called me and apologized. They said, "Honey, we support you completely. If the wedding is off, it's off. Maybe Jeff just isn't the right man for you." I got furious again—because by this time I'd decided I'd been being silly and the wedding was on after all. How dare they suggest Jeff wasn't the right man for me?
>
> I wish I could say this was the only incident like this during my engagement, but it wasn't. Before the wedding day arrived, my father told me to "behave myself," and my kid brother told me to "grow up." Worst of all, I overheard my mother telling my fiancé not to pay any attention to my "ravings" because it was probably my "time of the month." Talk about being mortified. The people closest to me were criticizing me, patronizing me, and talking behind my

back. This made me more anxious than ever, because
I thought, once you were about to get married, your
family would automatically treat you like a queen.

Margo's way of coping with stress was to try to spread it
throughout her whole clan. But after offering their sympathy
and understanding again and again, the job of tracking her
precipitous ups and downs became more than they could
handle.

Now, these three cases of anxiety overdrive may seem quite
pronounced. But they are far more common scenarios than
you might realize. And even brides-to-be who do not let their
anxiety carry them to quite such extremes will likely recognize
some of their own *tendencies* in these examples.

The important thing to remember is that you need not
give in to these tendencies. You can learn from your anxiety
rather than simply act from it. If you are willing to learn,
finding the *deepest underlying sources* of your anxiety can mark the
start of a profound emotional education.

To begin that education, you should know that one of the
primary sources of excessive Pre-Marital Syndrome anxiety is
spelled e-x-p-e-c-t-a-t-i-o-n.

WHAT DO YOU EXPECT?

It's said the Eskimos have a thousand words for "snow" in all
its variant forms. It seems there ought to be at least as many
words for "marriage." Because, in truth, when one individual
contemplates marriage—what it offers and what it requires—
he or she is often thinking along very different lines than
someone else might.

To help get your anxiety under control, ask yourself the

following question: Are you being honest about what it is you
desire and expect from your engagement, your wedding, and
your marriage?

Think about the three women whose stories were just
recounted. One of the reasons they went off the stress charts
is that they were unaware of certain deep-seated expectations
they were harboring. And those very expectations, though
unconscious, were nevertheless fueling their actions and attitudes.

In the case of Cyndi, the Righteous Romantic whose nuptial zeal alienated her co-workers and overburdened her fiancé,
we see a woman who consciously attributed her anxiety to a
need for a "perfect wedding." Deep down, however, she expected that the success of her marriage would hinge on her
ability to *be in control.*

In the case of Elise, the Teary Tester, we have someone
who thought her marriage would be jeopardized by her man's
being "set in his bachelor ways." Underneath this fear was her
belief that marriage meant *her partner should change his personality
to accommodate her.*

As for Margo, our Halfway Hysteric, she had an expectation of how marriage would change the way others viewed her.
In her mind, she believed her betrothal and subsequent marriage *would elevate her status in her own family*—even if she did not
behave like a mature adult.

These *unacknowledged* expectations caused this trio of altar-
bound women all manner of troubles. Because a hidden source
of anxiety went unnoticed, their stress became exacerbated.
Because these brides-to-be were unable to perceive how their
own secret motives fueled their behavior, they remained stuck
in their Pre-Marital Syndrome mode. And finally, because they
weren't listening to *themselves,* they were hard pressed to truly
listen to anyone else, including the very person they were
about to marry.

Is this any way to head toward marriage? Clearly it ought

not to be. But, alas, such fundamental ignorance is all too common. Many engaged women are simply not in touch with their many levels of hopes, intentions, and apprehensions.

THE IMAGINARY MARRIAGE

Although much pomp and circumstance surrounds the exchanges of formal vows and mutual promises during a wedding ceremony itself ("We'll love and honor, for richer or poorer, till death do us part"), it is a given among couples' therapists that such spoken "contracts" represent but the tip of the marital iceberg.

Each partner also brings to a marriage a grab bag of specific anticipations, beliefs, and plans of which they are aware, but which they have never said aloud to their mate ("Richer or poorer, hmmm. . . . Now that we're married, we'll do more saving and less spending").

Along with these conscious goals come the final category of schemes and dreams, the ones with which even the dreamer is not consciously acquainted. Often these have to do with global and critical relationship issues, such as gender roles and power divisions ("The only way for us to save more and spend less is for me to manage all the finances. After all, that's the way my mother and father did it.")

One can easily envision the bumpy road down which anyone harboring such expectations would have to travel once faced with a husband who had—as husbands so often do— a totally different scenario in mind. Well, this is the sort of journey you could be setting yourself up for even now.

Like the vast majority of brides-to-be, you are probably creating at this very moment an "imaginary marriage" in your heart and mind. Now, there's a lot of fun that goes along with such musings. But do yourself a favor and try to get a conscious handle on all your hopes and fears so that they won't undermine you during your engagement period or later. Try sorting out your imaginary marriage and finding out what you really expect with regard to some major issues that all married couples face.

UP-FRONT, BACK-BURNERED, AND OUT-OF-SIGHT EXPECTATIONS

Begin by listing what I'll call the Up-Front elements. These are the aspects of your hopes and plans that you verbally share with your fiancé and that you and he discuss openly (even if you don't necessarily always agree on them).

Next, list the things you anticipate getting from marriage or from your spouse that you are pretty clear about but that you haven't said aloud. These are your Back-Burnered expectations. If you need some inspiration, consider choosing from among the following critical areas:

Family planning
Financial planning
Career issues
Sex
Communication

For example, if you'd like to have two children and have told your fiancé so, that's an Up-Front expectation. If you think you should have them as soon as possible after the wedding, but have decided to remain silent about that for now, that's a Back-Burnered expectation.

So far, this may seem pretty simple. But now consider the third category of expectations for your imaginary marriage— the ones that contain your "secret" and "buried" answers to at least some of the following questions:

• *How will short-term and long-range decisions get made?* For example, will you negotiate, give in, take turns, or take over? Are you willing to compromise or do you expect your spouse to be the one who always bends?

• *What are your responsibilities in your marriage, and what are your partner's responsibilities?* For example, will one of you be "in charge" of the household chores? Will one of you be the "social director"? Will one of you be the sexual initiator? How will each of you be obligated to treat the other's family? How obligated are each of you to avoid future flirtations with the opposite sex, even if they're harmless?

• *What are your rights in a marriage and what are your partner's rights?* For example, will each of you have the right to spend time alone or with friends? Or will only one of you have this right—*you,* for instance? Do you think you should have the right to criticize anything about your spouse that you don't like? Does he have the same right?

• *How will your marriage be the same as (or different from) your parents' marriage?* Will you re-create their camaraderie—or their antipathy? Will you argue the way they argued, or will you refrain from arguing at all, because in your family all anger was bottled up inside? On the other hand, are you one of the many future newlyweds who swear that *nothing* about their marriage will resemble that of their parents?

• *In what ways is marriage supposed to make you "happy"?* Do you think your impending marriage "legitimizes" you as a worthy person, even if you never really felt that way before? Do you imagine your husband-to-be will take care of you the way your mother or father never did? Do you believe you'll never disagree, never feel a moment's restlessness, never have a single doubt once the knot is tied?

• *In what ways might marriage be just dreadful—the "worst mistake of your life"?* Are you afraid of losing your autonomy, of losing your freedom to make your own choices in life without having to consider another? Do you wonder if your man will "take you for granted" now that he's got you? Deep down, are you just about convinced he'll get fat and bald and fall asleep each night halfway through a *Columbo* rerun?

If my guess is correct, your mind is boggled right about now. How am I supposed to know what I think about all this, you may ask—*I only just got engaged.*

Right you are! The truth is if you knew all these things now, you'd be a nominee for the Marital Hall of Fame. Because, believe it or not, even the longest-married partners on the planet rarely reach a state of total awareness when it comes to the way they relate to their mate.

Human relationships are complicated, and marriage is one of the most complex of all. To some extent, all wives and all husbands have agendas hidden, at least in part, from one another and even from themselves. But this opening chapter was meant to alert you to the fact that yours are already at work, influencing the reactions you have to even *thinking* about marriage.

Though you cannot hope to know everything about your expectations, you can, with some introspection and perseverance, learn more than you knew before. You can also know that your husband-to-be is even now creating *his* own "imaginary marriage" operating at least partially on behalf of his Back-Burnered and Out-of-Sight expectations. So, if the two of you seem to be coming from different places at times, that may well be the reason why.

As you make your way through the remainder of your engagement, and through the rest of this book, try staying attuned to fleeting blips of free-floating anxiety, which may be your tip-off that there's an unacknowledged fear or fantasy nibbling away at your equanimity. Don't do anything drastic about it. Don't try to suppress it, and for now at least, don't feel you must confess it. Just *notice* your expectations, being as truthful with yourself as possible.

As we proceed, this book will address some of the more common fears and fantasies of future brides and investigate just how realistic—or unrealistic—they may be. You may well recognize some of your own expectations and learn something more about them.

Let's start by getting back to basics. You had just sighed a breathless yes to the much-awaited proposal. Now it's time to spread the news, and to encounter public opinion.

CHAPTER TWO

PUBLIC OPINION

Of all actions of a person's life, their mar-
riage does least concern other people; yet of
all actions of our life, 'tis the most meddled
with by other people.

——*JOHN SELDEN,* TABLE-TALK

Marie, a twenty-nine-year-old advertising copywriter, had a feeling her boyfriend, Don, a thirty-three-year-old commercial artist, was about to pop the question. Despite his usual spur-of-the-moment nature, he'd made advance reservations for Saturday dinner at a quaint country inn an hour out of the city where they lived. He'd requested she wear his favorite evening dress and he informed her he'd called ahead for a table by the fireplace.

She told her friends, "I think this is it." She even hinted broadly to her parents, joking that after Saturday they might be able to stop worrying about her turning thirty as a single woman. That Friday Don called and apologized profusely. He had to work Saturday to make a deadline at his magazine. The festivities were off.

The next night he suggested they meet for "a quick bite" at a neighborhood Chinese restaurant. Marie was wildly disappointed—until she opened her fortune cookie and read its message: "Will you marry me?" "Thank goodness," says Marie, "I didn't have to tell my family and friends I was mistaken."

Cynthia, a twenty-five-year-old teacher, was thrilled to be proposed to by Pete, the man she'd been dating since her senior year of college. Thrilled, because she loved him, to be sure. But also for another reason. It seems Cynthia's two suite mates in her college dorm, Patti and Laura, had already wed the men *they'd* been dating at school, and Cynthia had been maid (as opposed to *matron*) of honor at both occasions. Her single state had not gone unremarked upon by those brides and grooms, nor by the vast majority of wedding guests—most of whom evidenced a burning interest in Cynthia's "plight," along with plentiful free advice about how to get her malingering beau to say the long-awaited words. *("Give him an ultimatum!" "Tell him you want to see other people!" "Cry!")*

One Valentine's Day the increasingly chagrined Cynthia thought she was going to be disappointed yet again as Pete handed her a box from a local jeweler that clearly was not the right size for a ring. On opening it, she didn't notice, right off, that the watch it contained said "Marry me" on its face. When she finally did notice, the first thing she said was, "Oh, how wonderful." The first thing she *thought* was, "I wonder how soon we can tell Patti and Laura."

Whether we admit it or not, most of us are at least somewhat concerned about what others think of us and the person we plan to marry. At a certain point in our dating relationship, not only do our own expectations kick in, but so do theirs. When Aunt Lois asks pointedly, "Any news, dear?" she's not referring to the Middle East peace talks. And when our father starts wondering aloud about a beau's "intentions," he's not musing about whether or not he's going to run for Congress. And so, the pressure's on. Will he or won't he ask? Will you or won't you accept? And if you do, *what will everyone say then*?

The trouble is that getting totally wrapped up in the reactions of others to your happy news can lead to certain complications. Many new brides-to-be are so hyperconscious of the social pressure surrounding their engagement that they barely register what's happening themselves before they begin anticipating other people's reactions to it.

If you follow their lead, you may be setting yourself up for a fall. Because, as this chapter will show, even friends and family members who have seemingly been gearing up for your wedding since the first day you swapped your knee socks for panty hose may have some surprising reactions to your announcement of an honest-to-goodness betrothal. Your happy news may be a bit of a bombshell—even to those who eagerly awaited it. And if you don't understand *why* this is happening, you may be in for some unpleasant symptoms of Pre-Marital Syndrome—irritation bordering on outrage, tears and possibly hysteria, exacerbated doubts about your beloved or about the wisdom of your decision to wed, and, last but not least, guilt (because, much as you might like to, you can't tend to *other* people's feelings all the time).

On the other hand, if you are prepared, you can weather public opinion and keep its sometimes peculiar vicissitudes from draining you or undermining your relationship with your fiancé. Because "forewarned is forearmed," we'll explore some common public-opinion pitfalls and the fears and underlying fallacies that could potentially blow your reaction to them out of proper proportion.

THE IMPERFECT PARENTAL RESPONSE

Virtually all bridal guides recommend telling parents before you inform anyone else of your impending nuptials. They generally suggest sharing the news in person. If Mother and Dad live far away, they suggest that you tell them by phone, then schedule a visit as soon as possible. Of course, many engaged women feel the urge to tell their parents first, even if they are unaware that this is standard bridal protocol. It's a kind of instinctive reflex.

And not surprisingly, with all the intimate history and abiding affection between you and your parents, it's likely that your expectation is that they will express unmitigated glee and support at your news. But there's that word again: expectation. And once again, it may get you into trouble. For sometimes less-than-ideal reactions from one's mother or father are forthcoming. For example, here is what happened to Marie (who got engaged to Don via his fortune-cookie missive):

> The morning after my Chinese-restaurant engagement dinner I woke up early and dialed my mother's number first thing. It was busy because, as I later found out, she was already trying to call me—eager to know what had happened at the posh country inn I'd expected to go to. "Well, guess what, Mom," I said, and proceeded breathlessly to report what I thought of as Don's charming ruse, down to its last romantic detail. "Can you imagine how shocked I was?" I said. "Don't you think it was so *clever* of him to get that fortune-cookie thing all arranged?"
>
> I expected her to chime in on my praise for my creative boyfriend, but that's not what happened. Instead Mother asked, "You mean he didn't take you to a *fancy restaurant*? You mean he actually proposed to you at *Szechuan Garden*? My goodness, I never. What

did he make you order, the Early Bird Special?"

She went on and on like that, implying Don was a cheapskate or something. First I was speechless, then I started defending him and yelling at her: "I can't believe you're saying these things about my fiancé." I even remember thinking, "Well, *she's* not coming to this wedding." Needless to say, she totally changed my mood. What a morning.

Alas, Marie is not alone in getting an unforeseen and unwelcome response from one of the people whose good opinion and approval she genuinely valued most. To offer just one more of countless similar stories, here is what happened to twenty-seven-year-old Rita when she told her mother she was marrying a man named Larry, whom she'd been dating for nearly two years:

My mother had met Larry on, oh, I don't know, maybe twenty separate occasions. He always accompanied me to family holiday dinners, weddings, graduations, and such. He and my mother usually chatted a lot—she's pretty inquisitive—and I even remember them dancing on several occasions. She definitely knew him well.

But as soon as we got engaged, she couldn't seem to remember his name. All of a sudden he was *H*arry, and even once in a while *B*arry. She apologized, of course, when we pointed out her slip, but persisted in getting it wrong. She outdid herself one day when she had to introduce Larry to some cousins visiting from California whom he had never met. This time she didn't stop at simply switching a consonant. Instead, for some reason I'll never be able to fathom, she said, "I'd like you to meet my future son-in-law, Alan." Alan was a man I'd been engaged to when I was

twenty-four, someone I'd broken off with, and someone whom she said she'd never cared for. Was she
deliberately being thoughtless or was it just a blunder?
I was never sure, I only remember turning red as a
lobster, from embarrassment and fury.

As you've probably deduced by now, mothers are often
not the only ones who respond to the news of a daughter's
impending wedding with something less than a twenty-one-
gun salute. Here's what twenty-four-year-old Carol remembers
about her father's reaction:

My boyfriend, Anthony, decided he wanted to do
things the old-fashioned way. He told me he wanted
to speak to my father privately to ask for my hand in
marriage. I thought that was the sweetest thing I ever
heard, and I was sure my father would think so too.
So one night after dinner my father and Anthony went
to my dad's study for a man-to-man talk. When Anthony came back, he looked like he was in shock or
something. It seems my father had told him he wanted
to see his TRW credit report before he "made up his
mind." What in the world was my father thinking?

Like their own children, you, too, must be wondering what
these parents are thinking. Why was the behavior of these
parents so inappropriate? And what would you make of it if
your parents responded in a similar vein to your engagement
announcement? Would you pretend not to notice? (A Righteous Romantic might.) Would you burst into sobs at every
slight, and envision disowning your folks forevermore? (This
would be the path of a typical Teary Tester.) Or would you, in
classic Halfway Hysteric fashion, waffle between ignoring
them and shrieking at them?

You *could* try to understand what may be underlying your

parents' strange behavior. In truth it could be a combination of many things. For consider the plight of a parent, if you will. Their eagerly awaited baby daughter is born. They feed her, burp her, bathe her, change her, and applaud her fledgling attempts at walking and talking. In exchange for their love and care they receive back that brand of starry-eyed, blissful, exclusive love bestowed upon all-powerful parents by tiny children. Then things change.

The daughter goes to school, makes friends, spends a whole summer at Camp Runamok, and only writes home four times. When she comes back, she starts junior high school, starts wearing eye makeup, starts talking back to mom and dad—her former adored heroes!—as the stormy years of adolescence get fully under way.

The next thing they know, she's off to college, starting a job, beginning a life of her own. Then one day she says she's getting married. She begins to behold her fiancé with that brand of starry-eyed, blissful, exclusive love that once upon a time—it may suddenly seem like only yesterday—was *theirs*.

Thus, when you *say,* "Mom, Dad, I'm getting married," they may *hear:*

"You're no longer as important to me as you were."

or:

"Things between us will never be the same again."

or even:

"Good-bye, forever!"

And then, they may *think:*

"Who's this evil scoundrel who's stealing our baby away!?"

Granted, some parents act on such irrational thoughts and feelings more than others. But the fact is that announcing a betrothal to one's parents nearly always engenders in them what's known as *separation anxiety*. Though they may find their sudden sadness and alarm inexplicable, and even try their best to deny the existence of such emotions or cover them up, rest assured that part of them is, at the instant your words register, envisioning you as a helpless tot.

Your safest strategy is to stay alert to what's really happening and draw upon your understanding of the genuine love and concern behind their disconcerting and uncharacteristic behavior. Be as diplomatic as possible and try not to let them push your buttons.

You'll need your strength, for you still have your siblings to contend with.

SIBLING TRIBULATIONS

It is certainly not the case that *all* sisters and brothers proffer unsettling responses to the announcement of a sibling's engagement, yet I have heard such stories enough times to conclude that you should not be surprised if yours are among those who do. But there's often a difference between siblings and parents.

Sisters and brothers tend to irritate the bride-to-be in more subtle ways than mothers and fathers. They may not "forget" your beau's name or imply he's a tightwad. Indeed, they may not aim the force of their ambivalence at him at all, but rather at you. As many engaged women have found, an impending wedding often tends to ignite sister-to-sister or sister-to-brother conflicts reminiscent of the ones that were experienced in the years of childhood and adolescence.

Jessica, for example, was thirty-three at the time of her

betrothal. Her sister, Julia, was twenty-eight. Here is what she remembers:

> When we were growing up, my little sister was a pain. Even though she was five years younger, everything I did, she had to do too—only to a greater extent. When I teased my hair, she teased hers higher. Whatever "cool" slang I used as a teenager, she started to use all the time. I guess I shouldn't have been surprised that when I announced my engagement, she started telling everyone that she, too, expected to be getting married soon—even though this seemed to be news to her poor astonished boyfriend, who, it turned out, had had no intention of taking the plunge anytime soon. Before long everything I was picking out for my wedding was subject to Julia's commentary: "Oh," she'd say, "I'm going to have a dress just like yours, only I'll carry more flowers and wear a longer train." How competitive can you get?

Here is what twenty-two-year-old Marcia remembers about her brother, Bill's, prewedding behavior:

> All my big brother did was tease me. I thought he'd outgrown that. But as soon as I told him I was getting married, it was endless. "What is this, a cradle robbing?" he'd ask. "You're not old enough to be somebody's wife. You're still in terminal acne stage. What do you want for your wedding, a case of Clearasil?" Now, you could see how a little of this might be amusing, but I tell you, it really got obnoxious. It was the same old game he played when we were kids. It was like he was deliberately trying to get my goat, just to show he had that kind of power.

And here is what happened between thirty-year-old Daphne and her older sister, Lauren:

I'm a CPA, and at the time I became engaged, I was helping my widowed mother resolve some knotty tax problems. My sister, who had always been a nag, started laying a guilt trip on me: "Are you going to be able to plan a wedding and take care of this mess at the same time? I mean, that's not really wise, is it? What does Mom think of this? Isn't she worried?" Of course I got furious. I remember taking just so much and then blowing up. I started yelling, "No, she's not worried because she has *faith* in me—and because she's concerned about *my* life, too, unlike some people I know!"

And so we see the psychological shenanigans of a competitive kid sister, a big brother on a power trip, and an older sister who pounds away at a sibling's happiness with a hammer of guilt. What do they all have in common—in addition, that is, to the fact that their actions are contributing mightily to the stresses of a bride's Pre-Marital Syndrome?

Though it may surprise you to know this, they, too, are feeling a kind of separation anxiety. They'd probably deny it vehemently if you asked them about it, but you can bet that members of any family have a deep-seated investment in keeping things in their clan the same as they've always been.

Decades of study in the field of family therapy have revealed that members of a family unit are so invested in maintaining the status quo that they will undertake astonishing feats of emotional acrobatics in order to do so. Whenever there is a change—any change, even one ostensibly "for the better"— it is experienced as a loss. A loss of what is familiar—hence, a loss of what is comfortable.

When Julia cries "me too," when Bill teases, and when

Lauren carps, they are reenacting family dramas of yore, creating amazingly similar kinds of conflicts to the ones they had in the past. What's more, whether they know it or not, they are hoping to elicit from their soon-to-be-married sister a time-worn response—perhaps a whimper of capitulation, perhaps a roar of rage—that will prove she is still psychically engaged with them, though she is, literally, engaged *to* someone else.

At what is most likely an unconscious level, these needling brothers and sisters are trying to assure themselves that everyone's role in their family will remain the same. Families are delicate mechanisms, like well-oiled machines comprised of enmeshed cogs and wheels. Should one cog be displaced, the machine's routine movements are thrown out of whack.

In announcing one's engagement one is, in effect, heralding a displacement. For in a sense, a woman who is marrying may in fact leave a competitive sister who is not marrying behind. She may no longer endow a big brother with the power to taunt her, for his opinion may not carry such great weight with her now. She may indeed have less time to take on her assigned family role as "mother's helper" (and perhaps her worried sibling will have to take on that role herself!).

The family balance is at stake, and an engagement has tipped the scales. So a bride-to-be ought not be overly surprised if her siblings try to tip it back to starting position.

It will be easy—and on a gut emotional level very tempting indeed—to play along with your sibling's scripts. For you know just how they go. They push and you pull, they heave and you ho.

But, though your instincts tell you to play along, try attuning yourself to your best interests instead. Rather than labeling their actions "thoughtless" or "insensitive," see those actions as endearing (albeit annoying) attempts on your siblings' part to secure *your* role in the family drama. Then you may respond to them with a smile or a shrug instead of a tirade, and help keep your premarital stress down.

WITH FRIENDS LIKE THESE . . .

Now that you have told your family, of course, it is time to tell your friends, and it's likely that you are looking forward to these divulgences with much relish. Up to now you may have hinted, and they may have prodded. But now is the moment for the big revelation, and you expect their shrieks of ecstasy to pierce your awaiting ears.

So what if your family didn't give you the perfect response? You can't pick your family, right? But you picked your pals. And you fully anticipate their maximum nurturance.

Look up *friend* in your thesaurus and you'll find synonyms such as *advocate, ally, champion, cheerleader, promoter,* and *proponent.* Your gain is their gain, correct?

Then why do those same friends who've been singing the praises of your man suddenly imply you may be "too good for him"? Why do they seem more concerned with who gets to be maid of honor than with what you're feeling? Why do friends who have long lamented their single status now make the occasional comment about "the fundamental inequity that marriage holds for women"? Why do they question your motives, subtly implying you're settling out of fear of old-maidhood?

Wendy, who was thirty-four at the time of her engagement, recalls:

> I told Sandra, one of my closest friends for over ten years, that Mark proposed to me and that we were getting married that coming May. "Oh-ho, May what?" she asked. I told her May fifteenth. She said, "Well, you've beat your thirty-fifth birthday by just over a month. I guess you read that Yale study that said a college-educated woman has a greater chance of being stomped by a herd of elephants or something than getting married after *that.*" Well, needless to say,

I did not take this as the most positive comment she could make about my marriage—that I was just desperate. Since she was over thirty-five and single herself, I had to bite my tongue to refrain from yelling at her to look out for that herd of elephants right behind her.

There are many possible motivations that might underlie tactless responses from friends to your good news. Your single friends may fear that once you are wed, you will abandon them, socializing primarily with couples or holing up at home saving money for your dream house and eating tuna casseroles in front of the tube. Where your vision of the future is filled with tableaus of snuggly togetherness with your mate, they see a future of solo trips to Club Med, mourning the days when they had a reliable buddy with whom to make the rounds.

What's more—and we may as well face it—you cannot discount simple envy from coloring their reactions. Though this is perhaps not the most laudable of human emotions, it is, alas, among the most common ones. None of us is free from experiencing it, nor should we be surprised when we are the recipient of it.

As for your married friends, even they may not react with unadulterated enthusiasm. They, too, may fear seeing less of you in the future than they do now, or at least having the nature of their bond with you altered. For now and forevermore they must factor a new person, your husband-to-be, into the equation. They may feel dubious about sharing you, or anxious about the way your mate feels about *them*.

Knowing where your friends are coming from and understanding that their own insecurities may be speaking when they are responding to you should help you endure what can come off as as inconsiderate remarks. There's not much sense in blowing up if you can avoid it, for chances are your friends will shortly come around, putting their own agendas aside and becoming as excited as you are. That's good, for in the coming months you will *need* your friends as you make your way through the emotional obstacle course of Pre-Marital Syndrome.

THE *VERY* PUBLIC ANNOUNCEMENT

Assuming you have successfully steered clear of rupturing your relations with your family and close friends as they, deliberately or unknowingly, give vent to their mixed emotions, it is time to face your larger social circle. You or your family may consider placing an announcement in your local newspaper such as:

> *Mr. and Mrs. P. Worthington Fopp of Sulky Bottom, Maryland, have announced the engagement of their daughter, Phoebe Worthington Fopp, to Hubert Middlebrow IV, a son of Mr. and Mrs. T. S. Middlebrow of Hoppingfrog, Virginia. The wedding will take place in September.*

If such a proclamation is important to you or your loved ones, go ahead and revel in your celebrity. Just be aware that it may prompt a plethora of well-wishing calls from many people you barely know and several whom you wish you didn't. ("Say, Ms. Fopp, my polka band and I would love to play a few tunes at your blessed event.") So, keep your cool.

You may also wish to celebrate your betrothal by allowing someone to throw you an engagement party, a sort of miniature prelude to the grand event of the wedding itself. This is also a bride's prerogative. And it, too, can be fun, for it's not every day that a woman gets to be feted and hold court as the center of attention. Just know that this may entail facing not once, but twice, a mind-numbing array of details and decisions, not to mention navigating through a host of cheek-pinching, hair-tousling aunts, uncles, and grandparents who will offer *their* opinions—solicited or not—on your impending nuptials. So, keep your wits about you and eat some more yogurt dip whenever you're tempted to say something that will break the peace.

WHAT'S REALLY IMPORTANT

Certainly the majority of people who learn your news will wax enthusiastic about your good fortune and prospects for future happiness. This chapter is not meant to encourage you to keep your engagement a secret. Obviously you care deeply about the people in your life, and they care about you. So tell them! Just take with a grain of salt any odd bits of negativity, should they surface.

What's most important, however, is that you do not let anyone else detract from the most important thing of all, which is (you haven't forgotten, have you?) the relationship you have with the man you're going to wed. Indeed, "public opinion" is such tricky business that a bride-to-be is very vulnerable to incorporating the fears of others into her own perspective on marriage. Whenever you experience this type of anxiety, you should refer to the following four-point synopsis of the fallacies underlying your prewedding fears:

FEAR: "My family and friends aren't giving me the responses I expected. I should reconsider my plans. Maybe they know something about marriage, or about my man, that I don't know."

FALLACY: You are operating on the assumption that families and friends are not naturally prone to mixed emotions in the face of a loved one's rite of passage. You think anything less than full-out jubilation on their part bespeaks a horrible blunder on your part.

REALITY: *Of course* your family may have mixed feelings. This is only natural. They are reacting to the fact that your role in relation to *them* is in flux. Even if you've lived apart from your mother, father, and siblings for years, your marriage marks a more permanent parting—an ultimate reshaping of the way you relate to them. As for your friends, they, too, are unsure as yet how your relationship to them will alter. And they may be projecting their own problems onto you (perhaps they're lonely, or in a relationship they don't find as fulfilling as they'd hoped).

REMEDY: Your greatest danger is letting public opinion interfere with your true goals, desires, and needs. The most precious parts of your relationship with your mate are private; and the public and the private don't always mesh so well. You know—or should know—your fiancé better than anyone. Likewise, you should know your own motives for marrying better than anyone. If you don't feel this is the case, it's time for heart-to-heart discourse with your mate, along with some serious introspection. It's not time to adopt other people's uncertainties as your own.

On the other hand, it is not time *either* to disrupt relationships with people who are ultimately very important to you. Bear with them. Everyone should be entitled to have all their feelings.

You already know, if you're honest with yourself, that *you're* somewhat anxious and ambivalent. It goes with the territory. Why not allow that your family may be anxious as well?

It's unlikely that, in the long run, your family and friends do not want to share in your happiness. Give them a little time and pay attention. Soon you may notice more positive attitudes replacing dubious ones. At least they're trying. . . .

Now your news has been told, told, told again. It is time to proceed with the business at hand. And much business there is. For as the next chapter shows, brides-to-be are not long allowed to simply say, "I'm getting married!" Soon—very soon—people will want to know when, where, and how. The pressure to plan may grow so intense that you may start to wonder something else. . . .

CHAPTER THREE

THE PROSPECT OF
A WEDDING:
WHAT, WHEN, WHERE,
AND MOST OF ALL, WHY?

> A couple that can get through an
> engagement with all its etiquette
> landmines ought to find marriage a
> cinch.
>
> —MISS MANNERS' GUIDE TO
> EXCRUCIATINGLY CORRECT
> BEHAVIOR

Now that you've told everyone you're getting married, people
have a few questions. Or a few hundred. When's the big day?
Will the wedding be large or small? Where's the reception?
Sit-down or buffet? Who will perform the ceremony? Will you
write your own vows? Are you going to stand in a receiving
line, wear a blue garter, throw the bouquet, feed each other the
first slice of cake?

At first, all these questions are mildly amusing. What fun!
There's so much to think about, so much to choose from.
Planning the day of which you've always dreamed is going to
be the thrill of a lifetime. Nothing can compare!

But soon, very soon, you begin to feel twinges of nervousness. The myriad options available to you are overwhelming.
Any one decision seems to have a domino effect that you

imagine will not only affect every other detail of the wedding but will create enough emotional repercussions to last the rest of your married days.

Take for example a simple choice like: Will we wed in the afternoon or evening? Seems pretty basic, doesn't it? But wait a minute. If it's an afternoon wedding, can you wear a full-length dress? Can he wear tails? If it's an evening wedding, are you expected to have an open bar and one of those Viennese dessert tables that look like midnight snack time on the deck of the *QE II*?

If it's an afternoon wedding, will guests expect to bring their kids? And does that mean the groom's Aunt Doris will bring those rowdy twins who never leave home without their water pistols? But what if Aunt Doris hears she can't bring her brood to a more sophisticated after-dark affair? Will she ever speak to your fiancé again?

Okay, so let's try another decision. Something really simple this time. About something specific . . . say, photography. Are you going to pose for pictures or go with candid shots? Easy, candid. You hate those stereotypical portraits of bridal parties with frozen smiles and glazed eyes. But, not so fast. If you don't have posed photographs, you may leave someone out. Or capture them at an awkward moment, or in bad lighting. Someone important. Your best friend from junior high. The best man. Your mother! What will happen years from now when your own children look through your impromptu "candid" album of blurred visages and chopped-off hairdos and ask, *"Who's that?"* and *"Where's Grandma?"*

Already, you can feel your distress kicking in. The pressure, then tension—that sense of a great weight on your shoulders. You need help.

"No problem," you're advised. "You just need to get organized." So off to the bookstore you go to sweep up an armload of wedding planners (an armload because, right now, you can't even figure out which of *them* to choose).

And just like magic, you've got lists of popular wedding music, from Johann Strauss to John Denver. You've got wording for invitations. You've got comparison sketches of sleeves, bodices, necklines, and of headpieces, from "poufs" to "Juliet caps." You've got the pros and cons of assorted bridal fabrics, from tulle (okay for that ballerina look) to taffeta (good if you want an audible rustle). You've got illustrated options for bridesmaids and usher garb, and for bouquets, from "sprays" to "nosegays."

And since, as you'll recall, organization is the goal, you'll find the typical wedding guide filled with as many strategic-planning aids as would be needed to, say, plot a major corporate takeover or perhaps wage war in a small Central American country. You've got guest-list sheets and expense sheets, and logistics charts for housing out-of-town celebrants. You've got ceremony and wedding-site worksheets, invitation-proofreading checklists, flower checklists, procession-positioning charts, jewelry-purchasing guidelines, and the all-important wedding-day transportation worksheet (because it puts a damper on things if the bride or groom don't show up). You've charts for whom to tip and how much, and for keeping track of who gave you which gift. And if anyone needs your suggestions as to what gifts to get, you've got dinnerware, silver, and glassware checklists (don't forget that gravy boat and jelly spoon!) as well as one for basic linens and one for sundry appliances (you don't want to start your life together without an automatic espresso maker).

Last but not least, you've got a wedding-planning calendar where you can plot a day-by-day campaign with the zeal of Alexander the Great. And lest you fall behind, there is a master-planning checklist that itemizes what tasks are to be surmounted month by month.

All is laid out for you, leaving no stone unturned. A system like this should make you feel better, shouldn't it?

Then why doesn't it?

THE WEDDING CHORUS

Perhaps because someone seems to be looking over your shoulder at whatever move you make. Those inquisitive folks who, not long ago, besieged you with questions about how you were going to handle your wedding seem to have moved from curiosity to clairvoyance. They all look ahead in time and envision your wedding in some very particular way.

"I can see it now," says your mother. "The bridesmaids will wear teal. Uncle Ezra will play the oboe."

"*I* can see it now," your father stews. "Those caterers will bankrupt us unless you let me do the negotiating—and we limit the guest list to fifty."

"I'll be overjoyed to be your maid of honor," says your Cousin Celeste, to whom you *weren't* thinking of offering the job. "Your mother has such wonderful taste in clothing. I'm sure I'll look fabulous in teal."

Your friends, of course, have their scenarios planned out for you as well. "You're running off to Vegas, right?" nudges one who recalls her own wedding planning as an exercise in futility (ultimately this friend regrets having capitulated fully to her overbearing parents, who insisted on having everything *their* way).

"Oh, pleeease have one of those weekend weddings, with all those activities and parties and things," cajoles another friend (she emphatically wants a beau of her own and imagines "wedding camp" is a good place to find one).

Not to be omitted from this chorus of the ultraopinionated are your fiancé's family and friends. Your future mother-in-law, a major fan of Laura Ashley and all forms of chintz, envisions a country wedding. Your future father-in-law, now divorced from your future mother-in-law and living on a cabin cruiser with his new wife, Flo, invites you to let him perform the ceremony at sea. And your future husband's best buddy thinks it would be sensible for you to have a double ceremony with him and his fiancée in order to get a better deal on formal-wear rentals.

Everyone has their expectations (yes, there's that word again), and let us not forget those of the other half of your marital equation—your groom-to-be. Although sometimes it must seem like his sole function at this point in time is to annoy you. Perhaps because he has envisioned a wholly different sort of wedding than you have. Perhaps because he defers to you completely and maddeningly, responding to each query with, "Whatever you want, honey." Perhaps because he suddenly seems to be much more influenced by his family than you ever knew, responding to each of your decisions with, "Did you check that out with my mom, dear?" Or perhaps just because he's even more confused than you are and seems to be rapidly succumbing to prewedding paralysis of the brain.

At this point you feel pressured, beset with quandaries, burdened with responsibility, and irritated with those around you. What's more, you may feel completely inadequate when comparing yourself to illusory "ideal" brides—the ones whose calm, beaming faces and designer gowns adorn the front covers of your wedding planners and whom you imagine employ innate impeccable taste and flawless judgment to stage nuptial events of unsurpassed elegance.

Your anxiety level goes up several notches, and more than likely your preferred style of Pre-Marital Syndrome kicks in, suggesting to you a prenuptial schedule uniquely your own.

If you're the Righteous Romantic type, unshakably dedicated to the perfection of your wedding at all costs, your master plan may be unfolding like this:

Six months to a year before wedding
Start obsessing *now.*
Disengage your interest from all nonwedding-related activities.
Read everything ever written about wedding etiquette.

Ask everyone you know to recommend the absolute *best* caterers, florists, and so on.

Then ask them again if they know anyone even *better*.

Three to six months before

Fire caterer you've hired and retain another, more popular one who just had a cancellation.

Insist bridesmaids purchase $3,000 Dior ensemble, size 6—and instruct more amply endowed matron of honor to go on a diet.

Tune out anyone who wants to discuss emotions, including that size-10 matron of honor and, of course, your fiancé.

At fitting, berate yourself for forgetting the difference between a chapel-length and a cathedral-length train.

At stationers, throw fit at someone who says you could have gotten that engraved "effect" with raised lettering.

Two months before

Completely alienate future mother-in-law by explaining to her she has no taste.

One month before

Do likewise with your own mother.

Replace overweight matron of honor with slimmer pal.

Two weeks before

Turn a deaf ear to pleading fiancé who wants you to calm down and apologize to everyone.

Explain to him that he has no taste either.

One week before

Realize you're not on speaking terms with anyone, including the groom.

Gloss over this fact and fire the florist.

The day before
Have orchids Federal Expressed in from Hawaii at exorbitant cost.
Pace all night.

The day of the wedding
Buy new concealer for bags under eyes.

If you are a Teary Tester, one of those future brides who, in her months of engagement, dwells on little else besides potential future problems, your master plan may go something like this:

Six months to a year before wedding
Begin tormenting yourself with thoughts that you've just gotten engaged to the wrong person.
Lay in truckload supply of tissues and Visine.

Three to six months months before
Routinely confront your fiancé with each of his many flaws.
Disagree with him about everything, and take his objections as a sure sign he doesn't really love you.
Demand he change and then blow up when he doesn't.
Make excessive demands on anyone else you can think of.
Sob profusely while negotiating with caterers, florists, and so on.
Make as many scenes as possible.

Two months before
Awaken friends and family members late at night to express your doubts at every opportunity.

One month before
Discover your friends are getting unlisted phone numbers and that your family is considering doing the same.
Cry like a river.

Two weeks before
Go for final dress fitting and realize you've dropped another size.

One week before
Ignore your mother's pleas to eat something—anything!

The day before
Practice holding the drooping bodice of your baggy dress in place with safety pins.

The day of the wedding
Faint.

And lastly, if you are a Halfway Hysteric, one of those brides-to-be who vacillates between falling apart and straining to put herself back together again, your master schedule may look something like this:

Six months to a year before wedding
Get ultraorganized. Fill in all your checklists and charts.
Insist you don't need any help from anyone.
Change your mind about everything you've decided.
Rip up charts and checklists.
Insist you are a basket case who can't manage anything at all.
Enlist everyone with whom you're vaguely acquainted to help you pull through.
Tell them, "Never mind."

Three to six months before
Discover fiancé never told you about a woman he dated in seventh grade.
Decide you don't trust him anymore.
Tell everyone the wedding's off.

Make up with fiancé.
Tell everyone the wedding's on.

Two months before
Become incensed with fiancé for forgetting the anniversary of the day he first asked you out (and you turned him down).
Decide your romance is dead.
Ask your mother to let you move back home while you recover from your heartbreak.
Agree with your father that you'll be "Daddy's little girl" forever.
Receive life-sized stuffed koala bear from penitent fiancé.
Make up.
Tell your parents you overreacted.

One month before
More quarrels.
More stuffed animals.
Realize everyone around you is beginning to look a weensy bit bored and distracted when you shout and pout.

One week before
Now they're looking *very* distracted. In fact they don't seem to be taking you seriously at all.
Get hopping mad.
Then get a grip.
Throw yourself back into last-minute wedding details with a vengeance.
Tell yourself and everyone else that you'll be fine, just fine.

The day before
Wonder if you are developing a multiple-personality disorder.

The day of the wedding
March all your personalities down the aisle.
Have them say, "I do" and "I do too."

FEELING HELPLESS

If any of the foregoing "master plans" seems to be the way you are headed, you now at least know that you are in good company. Millions of engaged women have selected from this emotional menu year after year. We already know that one thing that drives them to such states of histrionics is their unspoken and unacknowledged fears about marriage itself. But there is something more. Along with anticipatory anxiety about what the future holds, there is genuine performance anxiety concerning the wedding event itself.

The bride-to-be wants things to go well, to be *right*, to be memorable and significant. This is no dress rehearsal, this is the real thing. And she knows (or at least hopes) that she won't get any chances to repeat this extravaganza in her lifetime.

That's cause enough for pressure. But, alas, there's more. The announcement of her forthcoming marriage seems to have given many people around her the idea that they now have a license to offer unsolicited advice, to intrude, and to manipulate. Part of the bride-to-be wants to oblige friends and family, who, after all, are usually acting out of love and sincere concern. But part of her feels tormented by their incessant butting in. Moreover, part of her wants to come to joint decisions with her future husband, while part of her has probably not yet really adjusted to the give-and-take dynamic that is ultimately the backbone of any solid marriage. If differences arise between the two of them, she generally feels at a loss.

Blend all these conflicting ingredients and you get an emotional soup called *helplessness*. Things seem out of hand, and getting more so by the minute. And the worried, harassed, confused bride may begin to think of herself as downright incompetent.

I suspect you will not be surprised to learn that feelings of helplessness are not high on the list of recommended boosts to mental fitness. Indeed one research study after another has shown that a sense of feeling in charge of one's environment and destiny, at least to some extent, is crucial for feeling relatively calm, grounded, and hopeful. When faced with help-lessness, some people turn angry, while some become de-pressed. The long and the short of it is you are simply not going to conjure up a positive attitude or get much pleasure out of things if you experience yourself as being at the mercy of others' whims.

The greater your sense of helplessness, the greater your tendency to suffer Pre-Marital Syndrome. The good news is you can fight your feelings of helplessness with a three-point strategy you may wish to remember as P.D.C.

P IS FOR PRIORITIZATION

Though the degree of outside input into wedding plans tends to vary, rare indeed is the bride who gets to orchestrate her wedding without the benefit of well-meant interference from family members. Even brides who live far away from their families usually receive long-distance dictums such as, "You *can't* get married on New Year's Eve in Minneapolis. It's freez-ing and your father's blood has gotten thinner from these Arizona winters!" But, in general, the closer you are to your family, both psychologically and geographically, the more such plaintive missives you will receive.

If you're like most soon-to-wed women—excited about starting a new family of your own, yet still tethered to your family of origin by love, respect and, let's be frank, a little bit of fear—you are probably torn. Part of you says it's time to take a stand and do everything your way. Another part remains dutifully eager to please.

To resolve your inner conflict, you must learn to prioritize. Consider which elements of your wedding hold the greatest significance for you. Perhaps you are very concerned about the menu (you're a vegetarian who doesn't want to violate your principles with Swedish meatballs). Perhaps you are *not* so concerned with what kind of floral arrangements go on the tables or whether your bridesmaids dye their shoes to match their gloves.

Once you have recognized what matters most to you, and what you are not willing to compromise on, consider compromising in areas of lesser concern. For example, Jill, who wed at twenty-eight, recalls:

> My mother was adamant that my husband and I have a large reception. And she insisted we arrive in a white stretch limo, which I thought was a bit much. She kept saying she didn't want people to think we couldn't afford it. That seemed shallow to me until she reminded me she and my father had been so poor when they married that their guests had to pay for their own dinners. To this day they felt they wanted to "make up" for that. I knew it was really meaningful for my parents to do my wedding up royally, but it was still my wedding. So to some degree I let them have a great time with the planning, but I insisted on keeping some things for myself and my fiancé to decide and manage exclusively. The party we did mostly their way, but the ceremony we did all our way. We were wed in front of close friends and immediate family only, wrote our own vows, selected all the music. And when it came to the honeymoon, we thanked my parents sincerely for their offer to send us to Hawaii, and drove off to Cape Cod for a week instead.

On a rather amusing note, Madeline, who was wed at twenty-seven, remembers:

> My father said we absolutely had to get married at his country club. He insisted the only reason he had stayed a member was so that he could see his daughter wed there. I knew it meant the world to him, and I knew it wouldn't be the *end* of the world for me and my groom. So we agreed. But then it turned out the club's chef was well known for his specialty, Chicken Kiev, and that's what my dad wanted served. But I said, "I am not having food that *squirts* at my wedding dinner. Case closed." We had poached salmon. Small victories are worth a lot.

Many women may feel these brides compromised too much. Others may find such concessions more palatable. The point is to decide what is right for you and then express your needs.

To do this, be *resolute yet diplomatic*. You can kindly and gently set limits on your parents' interventions and on those of well-meaning friends, future in-laws, and so on if you:

• Are clear in your own mind about what matters most to you
• Express those needs firmly, yet calmly
• Are alert to what matters most to others—and why
• Remain somewhat flexible in those areas

In addition, remember that your loved ones are just that— *loved*, even when they are being demanding. So:

• Make an effort to hear and respond to their underlying good intentions, *especially* when you disagree with them about the specifics of your wedding

• Try to maintain a lighthearted attitude
• Resist giving in to feelings of grandiosity (it's a celebration you're planning, not an intergalactic space mission)

Your wedding is your wedding, and you are, it is true, under no obligation to please anyone or do anything. *Absolutely* the most important people to please are you and your fiancé. But if striking a thoughtful balance when it comes to certain arrangements is tolerable and will make things run a great deal more smoothly, you would be wise to do so.

D IS FOR DELEGATION

Prioritizing, as it happens, gives you another advantage in battling excessive Pre-Marital Syndrome. You may have noted that the typical "master schedules" for Righteous Romantics, Teary Testers, and Halfway Hysterics include a penultimate burnout factor. Just before the wedding, the stress level, though already high, escalates precipitously. Fatigue, puffy eyes, and malnutrition rule the day. At this point it is practically all one can do to propel oneself toward the altar as if on automatic pilot, wondering what happened to the "happiest day of your life" concept.

If you follow your prioritization with *delegation,* however, this need not occur. Once you have figured out what is truly important to you, you will know what is really important for you to be in charge of. As for the rest, you may feel free to assign it out to friends and family members, who will likely be pleased and flattered that you asked.

One prioritization-delegation system that works very well is to sit down and assign a number, on a scale of 1 to 10, to each feature of your wedding. Give 9s and 10s to the aspects that concern you most and that you are certain require your personal supervision. Consider "farming out" anything that merits an 8 or below.

There are a number of ways of matching a task with a caring, competent supervisor. For instance, you can put the people who are most adamant about a feature of your wedding being a certain way in charge of getting it that way. They'll have a vested interest, after all. So if your mother is inordinately concerned with the way your invitations look and you attribute to this aspect of your nuptials slightly less importance, you may choose to delegate ordering, phrasing, and fretting over the invitations to her. There's a certain justice to this type of matchup that many find appealing.

On the other hand, you'll need to use your best judgment to prevent mismatches. It doesn't *always* follow that because someone is extremely opinionated in an area that they know much about it. You're intimately acquainted with your family members and friends. And for the most part you know where their talents lie. It would be foolhardy not to delegate certain chores accordingly. Thus, despite the fact that your father, the Perry Como fan, has been haranguing you for weeks with the rhetorical question, "Shouldn't I know how to pick out music for a wedding by my age?" you may wish to delegate such selections to your brother, Fred, the concert violinist. Even if he is not as eager, you may well find Fred willing—and doubtless able.

Of course delegation sometimes sounds easier than it is. Righteous Romantics dislike the idea of diminishing their sphere of influence in any way. Teary Testers sometimes confuse delegation with surrender, becoming so distraught that they relinquish all of their bridal leverage and let others seize total control (in weddings, as in all other areas of life, power abhors a vacuum). And Halfway Hysterics, swaying on their perennial emotional seesaw, often allocate tasks to willing helpers when they feel they're drowning, only to change their minds and reclaim those same chores when they come up for air (much to the chagrin of the helpers who proudly took their assignments to heart).

Delegation takes determination. It also takes trust. But

these are some of the things that marriage requires, too, so you may as well get into the habit.

C IS FOR COMMUNICATION

In all the planning and scheduling, of course, you must not lose sight of one very important thing—that being the reason you are going through all of this in the first place. You are getting *married,* remember? Moreover, you are getting married to a particular man because you love him.

Right?

But chances are you may have lost sight of that amid all the brouhaha surrounding your gala event. Indeed, some women report arriving at a point in their wedding preparations where dealing with their future husband's opinions—or lack of them—seems like just another burden. You don't want to join the ranks of such women. But to prevent yourself from doing just that, you must employ the third element of the P.D.C. solution: communication.

If your fiancé is exhibiting signs of "wedding withdrawal," that is, trying to ignore the whole matter of your joint command performance and leaving all decisions up to you, consider whether it may be because you have been ignoring *him.* Do not neglect to solicit his input on matters large and small. And most importantly, once you have solicited it, do not neglect to consider it. For, as you ought to learn sooner rather than later, communication consists of two basic elements: talking and *listening.* Most brides-to-be, whether Righteous Romantics, Teary Testers, or Halfway Hysterics, have little trouble with the first part. For when anxieties are in overdrive, long-winded soliloquies come easy. The listening part, however, is tougher to manage, as it requires calming down long enough to let someone else's message penetrate one's overactive brain.

Try it. It's really not so bad. In fact, you may find that your spouse-to-be has some rather good ideas about what ought or oughtn't to be done where your wedding planning is concerned. You may find that understanding his concerns helps *you* to prioritize; and you may discover, happily enough, that he is even ready, willing, and able to have some tasks delegated his way.

Of course, you may find you and he are in complete disagreement about matters both major (like whether a small wedding consists of 15 guests or 150) and comparatively minor (like whether it's practical to use the colors of his high school football team as your reception motif). That's where communication becomes truly important.

If you disagree on a deeply significant matter, listen carefully, for you may find you have uncovered the tip of an iceberg. He wants to be married by a rabbi. You already contacted a minister. You each *assumed* the other knew how important it was to you to be married under the auspices of your own religion. Suddenly you are aware of Back-Burnered expectations each of you has been harboring. Now you know that you are likely going to have to resolve not only this particular issue but others stemming from the joining of two people with different faiths. (How, for example, will you celebrate the holidays? How will you raise your children?)

It is by no means too soon to begin to talk things over, as patiently and clearly as you can. Don't try to find solutions to all your wedding-inspired dilemmas at once (an unrealistic "stormtrooper" approach that never works in any case). But do try to understand the motivation behind what your groom wants. Is he more involved in his faith than you had realized? Is he concerned with not offending his family? Then try to find a specific solution to your immediate quandary. Would he, for instance, consider a dual religious ceremony? As for yourself, express your needs to the best of your abilities. Is marriage by a minister a priority for you, for your family, or both?

It's possible that if your mate doesn't know these things about you, nor you about him, it is because you have both been nurturing the fallacy that you had already made your viewpoint known—though in fact you had not been clear. Next time, perhaps, you will not behave as if your partner was a mind reader, and you will be more straightforward about what it is you desire or require (voicing your expectations as the Up-Front kind).

If you disagree on a relatively insignificant matter—one that has to do with a ceremony or reception detail as opposed to the wedding's overall tone, size, or style—your wisest course of action is to recognize that it is indeed insignificant. You and your future husband may wish to do a joint prioritization scale and rate your differing alternatives accordingly. For example, if he wants to have Elvis's rendition of "Love Me Tender" played as your recessional and you wanted Handel's *Water Music,* assign a numerical value to each preference. You may find that, for him, having Elvis be a part of your wedding merits a 9.5 (hey, he *worships* Elvis). You'd give *Water Music* about a 6. In that case, it would be politic, and relatively painless, for you to go with Elvis and put your personal stamp on other areas of the celebration.

But keep in mind also that such logistical accommodations might not be enough to quell the bickering that could potentially arise around wedding-related decisions. Oftentimes brides- and grooms-to-be will disagree vociferously about everything from cuisine to the fine points of attire in order to mask the fact that they are on edge or at odds about other things. This, too, is a reason to focus on clear communication.

A quarrel over canapés or crudités may be an expression of fear of the loss of autonomy ("If I give in on asparagus spears, I'll have to give in on everything!"). Likewise, a flamboyant argument over the cut of a tuxedo may indicate a panic at the enormity of the upcoming commitment ("I never thought I'd look like one of those miniature people on top of the cake. *What am I doing?*") If you're not sure why you're both getting so hot under the collar over "nothing," ask your spouse and, equally important, ask yourself what's really going on.

You may find that beneath the disagreement you are in accord concerning some essential facts of premarital life: you're both scared silly.

TEN REASONS TO ELOPE

None of this is likely to prove especially easy. You are about to undertake one of the most important rites of passage in your life, and on top of that you are in charge of wining, dining, and entertaining a group of people who are especially important to you and to your mate. Even with the use of prioritization, delegation, and communication, there will likely be moments when you feel utterly consumed with the *what, when,* and *where* of your wedding. If you are like most future brides, you will at least occasionally start to ponder the *why* of what you're doing. Why orchestrate a wedding when you can skip town, hop a jet, and get married under a palm tree, or cab down to City Hall and say "I do" during lunch hour.

An elopement is, of course, a time-honored alternative to a conventional wedding. If you and your groom have simply had enough of charts, checklists, and schedules, you may jointly decide to throw up your hands and cry uncle. That's your prerogative. After all, an engagement is a promise to wed, not necessarily an obligation to mount a major production.

If you're really going to go through with an elopement, you'll need to mitigate the letdown of your family and friends. To assist you, here are ten perfectly viable rationalizations for eloping:

• *The Safety Factor:* Uncle Theodore and his brother, Bert, haven't spoken in fourteen years. The last time they encountered each other, at Great-aunt Blanche's funeral, there was that horrible wreath-throwing incident. A reunion at your wedding could cause a full-scale rumble.

• *Philanthropy:* The cost of even a modest wedding rivals

that of sending a busload of inner-city kids to summer camp or buying a new set of uniforms for the town band. It's not very "nineties" to be so self-indulgent.

• *Cardiovascular Concerns:* Wedding cakes are high in cholesterol. That's probably what killed Great-aunt Blanche. . . .

• *Endangered Species:* The proper execution of wedding etiquette requires several reams of high-grade paper for invitations, reply cards, announcements, and thank-you notes. Paper requires tree chopping, and tree chopping means fewer nooks and crannies in which a spotted owl may nest. You've seen pictures of those spotted owls, and they're downright *adorable*. Far be it from you . . .

• *Sports:* Hard as you tried, you could not come up with a date for your wedding that did not coincide with a major sporting event. Between NBA play-offs, the World Series, and Bowling for Dollars, there's always some competition that's of paramount concern to the sports fanatics in your family. You wouldn't think of depriving them of live coverage . . . because watching the video is just never the same.

• *Ophthalmology:* You've heard overexposure to flash bulbs can cause retinal damage. Why subject your loved ones to the dangers of camera glut?

• *Dentistry:* Likewise, you seem to recall reading somewhere that smiling too much could lead to temporal mandibular joint syndrome. There's an awful lot of smiling at weddings, and TMJ can be acutely painful. Why risk it?

• *Anthropology:* Prenuptial research revealed to you that Hindus exercise the greatest care in choosing a favorable wedding month. You, on the other hand, picked one when the country club had a cancellation. That turned out to be May, which the ancient Romans, not to mention the Celts, thought inauspicious for marriage. The ancient Greeks—yes, those *very* smart people who gave the world democracy—thought January was the most favorable month to wed. So you simply *had* to elope during your Barbados vacation.

• *Astrology:* On top of that, you realized the date for which your nuptials were set was a celestial disaster. Your moon would have been in Pluto and Mercury would have been in retrograde. Yikes! You had to run off and marry while Jupiter aligned with Mars.

And finally:

• *Sanity:* You'd like to start your marriage off with a small vestige of the mental health you enjoyed before you ever got engaged at all. But planning a wedding nearly put you over the edge. Given the choice of an elopement or a lobotomy, you chose the former.

Now you have plenty of justifications if you need them. But, what the heck, you probably won't use them. You know you'll probably regret it if you don't do your wedding up "right." Despite all your protestations, secretly you'd like a fairy-tale day—a tasteful, reasonably relaxed event at which you look and feel wonderful and your loved ones have a great time and behave themselves. You can have that, if you remember to face the fears behind your Pre-Marital Syndrome stress, and temper them with a dose of reality. So keep the essence of this chapter in mind:

FEAR: "Planning this wedding is really frustrating. I never thought it would be like this. I'm too much of a wreck to get married at all!"

FALLACY: Our society has a penchant for playing up the period of planning one's wedding as a time of unmitigated exuberance. If you don't feel as enraptured as the models on the covers of bridal magazines appear to feel, you doubt and criticize yourself. You think, "I don't have much of an aptitude for this!"

But those cover models are merely posing. You

are in the thick of things. And there's quite a difference. Give up the myths and face it: Wedding planning is often an exercise in frustration.

REALITY: Wedding planning is also a big responsibility. If you're like most engaged women today, you've already got plenty of other responsibilities on your plate. But guess what? You'll soon have another major mission. Together with your husband, you will be creating the foundations of a relationship that you hope will endure the ups and downs of a lifetime. You think you know frustration now? Wait until later. Marriage requires a high degree of compromise, diplomacy, flexibility, and tolerance. Thus all the skills you are mastering now with relation to your wedding will be of invaluable service down the road.

REMEDY: In wedding planning (as in marriage) figure out what's most important to you and let some less important matters go. Don't feel you have to do everything yourself, for though you may think that's selfless, it's really selfish.

Express your needs, but learn to listen to the needs of your mate. Try to discover *why* he wants what he wants so that you can view things through his eyes. Surely you will still disagree from time to time, but be prepared to let those differences of opinion instruct you as to what's really meaningful to each of you.

Keep monitoring and clarifying marital expectations as you go along rather than sweeping them under the carpet of planning mania. Remember that, very often, disputes about seemingly minor details are a hook on which to hang deeper anxieties.

And, speaking of hooks on which to hang deeper anxieties, proceed to the next chapter to consider one of the largest such hooks of all time: Money.

CHAPTER FOUR

MY GOD, HE'S A TIGHTWAD . . . AND OTHER REVELATIONS

For money has the power above
The stars and fate to manage love.
—*SAMUEL BUTLER*

You may have already noticed that one crucial feature of your planning went unaddressed in the preceding chapter. I am referring to the instruction that, as typically presented by bridal guides, reads simply, "Discuss budget."

To the uninitiated this may conjure up visions of an engaged couple sitting down over a snack while calmly trading concerns and suggestions on the subject of money and their wedding. ("Say, honey, I don't want to go overboard." "Me neither, how about we spend seventy-five dollars per guest and no more?" "Fine, sweetie!")

Those who have seriously begun to make plans, however, probably already recognize this "elementary" task for what it is—at best a major obstacle on the road to wedded bliss; at worst an invitation to full-blown disaster in their relationship. ("What does he mean, he doesn't want to go overboard. What a cheapskate!" "What does she mean, seventy-five dollars a head? What a spendthrift!" *"The wedding's off!"*)

Why all the woe surrounding money matters? Well, why not? Money is one of the most potent substances ever created. It's powerful in an actual sense, in that you can't get through a single day without it. In addition you'll soon realize that money is extremely powerful in an emotional sense.

In the premarital state you should be aware that you are especially susceptible to money's capacity to overwhelm, fluster, rankle, and incite. On the most basic level the sheer volume of money-related decisions one must make with regard to a wedding sets the mind reeling.

A quick perusal of your bridal planner reveals the startling number of items that will require somebody's bank balance to dwindle. Sure, you'd thought of the obvious ones from the first—food, liquor, musicians, your dress. But there seem to be about a million other expenses that you maybe hadn't thought of—from the minuscule (the matches, the cake boxes, the corsages for mothers) to the major (the rings, the photo proofs, the attendants' gifts); from the essential (the license, the blood tests, the invitations) to the extravagant (the ice sculpture, the caviar bar).

On top of this, you need to be concerned with just whose bank account is going to be debited for what. Alas, though various planning guides include explicit lists of which payments fall to the groom or groom's family (from the clergy member's fee to the honeymoon) and which to the bride or bride's family (from the rental of the aisle carpet to the reception site, food, and entertainment costs), myriad extenuating circumstances may prevent such a traditional division of expenditures from applying to your situation. Perhaps:

- Neither you nor your family can afford it
- Neither the groom nor his family can afford it
- You and the groom are quite solvent and don't wish any financial help from your families

• You and the groom are broke—but still don't wish any financial help from your families

• You are flush and the groom is broke, but he wants to pay for the reception—at Wendy's

• The groom and his family are all flush—but they think Wendy's is a neat idea

If none of the above fits your scenario, you may be in the most familiar set of circumstances of all: the one where everybody's got *some* money to spend and is somewhat willing to spend it, but no one can seem to agree on how much of whose should be spent on what. That's unnerving because of the logistical snags that are created, but also because such disagreements feed into the anxieties of the three prevalent Pre-Marital Syndrome styles.

Righteous Romantics, who want the best of everything, often become enraged at any tasteless oaf who does not share their appreciation of the finer (and higher-priced) things.

"I insisted on having a black-tie affair for our wedding," recalls twenty-nine-year-old Terri. "It was within our means to do something elegant. My fiancé was not so sure about this plan, though. He wanted a more casual afternoon event. He said some members of his family might not feel comfortable in formal clothes, but I thought that was just an excuse to save money. I was adamant. I insisted on black tie. I kept saying, 'Well, we can afford it, so why not? Why do you want to cut corners on the most important day of our lives?' It was only when his family showed up looking pained in their gowns and tuxedos that I realized I probably should have reconsidered when he'd asked me to."

Teary Testers often mistake a financial no from the groom's side as signifying "I don't love you anymore."

"Several months before our wedding," says thirty-one-year-old Nina, "my fiancé and I were at a very glamorous party given by the company he works for. At that party I began talking to a woman who was famous for her floral arrangements at society weddings. She told me she bought from flower markets all over the world and worked with the most beautiful blossoms in season to prepare the most opulent arrangements. I was determined we should use her and introduced her to my boyfriend by saying so. He turned ghostly pale at the time. Later he told me there was no way we would be using this lovely lady's services. She was completely out of our price range. What a fight we had that night, and then I moped for weeks. I couldn't believe he was being so stingy, after I had *promised* this woman and all. Obviously he just didn't really care about me. Months later I read about a wedding where the flowers had cost close to what we make in a year. Guess who did the arrangements?"

And let's not forget those Halfway Hysterics, who alternately come down on the side of financial splurging or financial purging (usually the opposite of whatever their befuddled groom is recommending at any given moment) as they try to make up their minds about just *what* it is they want, anyhow.

"We had so many fights about money, it was ridiculous," confesses twenty-seven-year-old Leigh. "My groom wanted to splurge on things I thought we should save on. I mean, why have an orchestra when you can have a disc jockey? And I wanted to spend on things he thought were frivolous—but would you call invitations done by hand frivolous!? Anyway, when it began to look like we'd never agree on anything, I got that old familiar feeling again—like maybe this was all going to fall apart at the last minute. Then I'd go through a phase where I'd get really frugal, because I was hedging my bets. Once when we were quarreling, I remember thinking that I would go to one of those shops where you could rent a designer dress for one occasion and then bring it back. I thought, why invest in a dress of my own when we're probably going to break up anyhow. Then we made up, and I panicked, 'Oh, God, I have no dress.' "

Of course the delicate matter of money is an ongoing issue between any bride and groom, and the wedding is just the proverbial tip of the iceberg. Virtually every practical decision you make at this stage of the game involves finances. Where will you and your husband-to-be honeymoon? Where will you live? How will you furnish the place where you live? And what about after settling down? Suppose *he* thinks you should put all your money in a joint checking account—and *you* think, "Not a chance!" You'd rather die than let him know how much you pay for a facial and an eyebrow wax.

Countless studies have shown that nothing is as likely to set two lovebirds off on a mutual tirade as the very touchy question of money. You never thought about this part when you fell for his crinkly dimples and impressive IQ, did you? But the truth is that you two, like any couple that weds, are forming a financial "corporation" of sorts. Unfortunately, unlike two parties in a formal business merger, men and women in love matches often start off their period of engagement with little idea about one another's "fiscal policies," that is, the attitudes they harbor deep down when it comes to matters of finance.

Does it pain him to pay bills? Or does he lose sleep unless he pays them the day they arrive? Does he procrastinate where you obsess (or vice versa)? Do you know precisely what your bank statement might read at any given moment, while he'd rather face a rabid pit bull than balance his checking account?

You simply may not know much of this when you agree to be his bride. For chances are he has been (like you) on best behavior, financially speaking, during your period of courtship. But now your impending wedding is compelling you to share some financial decisions and responsibilities—and, as a kind of side effect, the proverbial cats are let out of their bags.

This is tricky business, and it's understandable why many engaged women come to think that *budget* should be a four-letter word. But if you and your partner are going to discuss money with any semblance of reason before your wedding, or for that matter after, there are two essential truths with which you should become acquainted: (a) To some degree virtually everyone is quirky when it comes to money; and (b) couples often accentuate each other's financial eccentricities.

QUIRKY, MOI?

Now, before you start protesting that you are most certainly not included in the aforementioned group of "virtually everyone" (though you may readily admit your fiancé is!) consider that there are perfectly good reasons why all of us are susceptible to a certain degree of money madness. Think of these reasons as the "three Cs": *character, conditioning,* and (the last actually a double *c*) *cultural contagion.*

What's meant by *character* is that nearly everyone associates money with some emotional quality. Although at its most utilitarian level money is a commodity we exchange for goods and services, in the psyche it becomes much, much more. People are wont to associate money viscerally with such things as power and control, freedom, self-esteem, security, love, and happiness. And as strange as it may seem, some even associate money with feelings of gloom or shame (perhaps you have run across those people who are embarrassed by money matters and seem to behave as though they are trying to make all their assets go away). Indeed, more than a few us of are apt to associate money with a combination of both positive and negative feelings and harbor a deep-seated ambivalence toward it which we may act out in, say, splurging on some things and scrimping on others, or going through alternating periods of money obsession and money avoidance.

Why we make such emotional associations with money is a somewhat complicated matter. To some extent it is simply because money, so omnipresent in our daily life, serves as a convenient, blank projection screen onto which we may project our assorted worries and concerns about who we really are. If we experience ourselves as having a lack of something (not enough affection, authority, peace of mind, or personal attractiveness), we might imagine that by having more money that "hole" can be plugged. If we feel we are fundamentally undeserving of all we *do* have, however, we can mismanage our money so that problem after problem is created and much of life's spontaneity and fun falls by the wayside while we attempt (futilely) to straighten out our pecuniary affairs.

But we don't generate all of our own money attitudes. Many of them evolve out of the second *c*—*conditioning* via our family background. Parents impart money messages to their children in countless ways. They may, through word and deed, stress thrift by teaching that "a penny saved is a penny earned" or that "money doesn't grow on trees." They may encourage dreaming by insisting, "Someday our ship will come in." They may induce a deep trepidation where money is concerned by instructing that it is "the root of all evil." Or they may encourage gender stereotyping by conveying the notion that making money is "man's work" or that "women have no head for figures."

In response to parental money attitudes a child may spend a lifetime re-creating them. Thus if you had a parent who lived in fear of financial catastrophe, you, like that parent, may be prone to hoarding. But parent-child relationships being what they are (which is to say *very* convoluted), many children grow up to react against the financial dicta of a parent. A child who is the defiant, rebellious type may overspend or take truly imprudent financial risks to prove just how different he or she is.

The third and final *c,* the double one, refers to the *cultural contagion* that takes place when someone is profoundly influenced by attitudes that are emblematic of his or her particular era or immediate community. Someone who came of age during the Great Depression is likely to be more frugal, for example, than a baby boomer. Someone who grew up in a very status-conscious neighborhood is more likely to display a bent for a "keeping up with the Joneses" type of consumerism. Someone who works in a highly competitive profession where salary is synonymous with clout is likely to equate self-worth with the bottom line of his or her financial statement.

Given all this, it's small wonder that practically no one can boast a totally pragmatic, logical, conflict-free relationship with money. Perhaps now you are ready to admit that you, like the rest of us, may be vulnerable to a *few* eccentricities. But if you still think your fiancé is the only quirky one of the two of you, read on. For something interesting is about to happen to your money attitudes, whatever they may be.

THIS WAY AND THAT

As you'll recall, the second essential truth about money that brides-to-be ought to bear in mind is that couples often accentuate each other's financial quirks. There are several reasons behind this dynamic as well.

I sometimes give seminars on the topic of money and relationships, and one of the questions I am asked most often is "Why do spenders always seem to end up with savers?" If you'll think about it for a few minutes, mentally running down the list of couples you know, you will see that this is so often true, it seems downright uncanny. Spenders *do* seem to pair up with savers, and what's more, procrastinators link up with compulsive types, risk takers tend to pair up with fiscal conservatives, and dreamers (who have big fantasies even if they don't have big bank balances) seem to pair up with schemers (who are busy keeping track of every dollar).

In some cases these matches are polarized from the beginning and may be explained by the old adage "Opposites attract." Remember, most of us do harbor some ambivalence where money is concerned, which means that though we function primarily in one dominant money mode (e.g., saver), at least some small part of us is attracted to the idea of spending. When we see a spending attitude embodied in someone else, we may secretly admire it, thinking, "I wish I could indulge myself as this person does." Likewise if our dominant money mode is spending, we may secretly admire the self-control and restraint evidenced by a saver.

But please note: Though we may at some level admire our "opposite," we also *fear it.* So, once in an ongoing relationship with a person who harbors a largely "alien" money attitude, we say, "Hey, that's not mine! I don't understand it. I don't like it." We may go out of our way to find fault with it, because it is so threatening.

Of course, it's not always the case that people who marry embrace two opposing money attitudes. You may be a saver betrothed to another saver, for example. But if that's the case, you've likely already noticed something remarkable occurring. One of you is probably emerging as the bigger saver of the two, and the other, by comparison and by a kind of default, is looking like—and taking on the role of—the spender.

Amazingly, when two individuals come together to form a new whole, they tend to part ways and polarize over money even if their differences were not so great to begin with. This is so very common because conflicting attitudes that seem to come with the territory of money now have a more clear-cut forum in which to be acted out. When you are single, you get to deal with ambivalence all on your own, and that ambivalence may be only subtly experienced or expressed. When you are engaged, and later wed, the relationship itself can exemplify ambivalence, with the two parties involved each playing out one side of the coin, as it were.

So, where both you and your fiancé may have been in agreement at the start of your wedding planning that you would host a relatively modest affair; you may find that he is veering more and more toward cost-cutting measures (he knows a warehouse where you can save big on bulk quantities of frozen cocktail wieners), whereas you are leaning more and more toward signing up for those "little extras" that will make your day memorable (how much could one little swan-shaped ice sculpture hurt, after all?).

MONEY AS A MASK

To add further complexities to the dynamics of couples and money, there is also the fact that one of the reasons couples have so many fights about money is that a number of those quarrels are not really about money at all. Rather, they may be about such issues as:

- Who is more dependent on whom
- Who has more power in the relationship
- Who trusts (or mistrusts) whom
- Who is more responsible than whom
- Who loves the other one more
- Who is withholding
- Who is self-destructive
- Who is feeling guilty
- Who is feeling insecure

During the period of engagement many of these issues will arise as couples feel their way around the beginnings of a long-term committed relationship, carting their Back-Burnered and Out-of-Sight expectations in tow. At the same time, however, there is this pressing matter of the BIG EVENT looming, not to mention the BIG BUCKS it will cost. It's not surprising, then, that much of what's simmering below the surface of Pre-Marital Syndrome bubbles up in the guise of money issues.

Once you progress to the married state, of course, the emotional issues around dependency, power, trust, and so forth remain. But there are money decisions aplenty with which to cover them up if a couple is in the habit of using money in this fashion. Before long it may seem that you are angry about money just about all the time (because you simply won't acknowledge being angry—let alone sad or anxious— about anything else!).

It's best to nip this bad habit before it's in full bloom— which is to say before you and your partner tie the knot at all. But how can you begin?

TALKING MONEY

There is simply no other way to begin than by dialogue. In order to relieve premarital stress and to lay the foundation for a strong and healthy marriage, you and your fiancé need to do something besides speaking about money in terms of its specific allocations for your wedding. You need to speak about what money means to each of you and about what financial attitudes you hold as a result of that meaning.

Excuses abound for not being forthcoming about such delicate matters. Many people are loath to discuss their financial life with anyone, including—perhaps especially—their betrothed. Some believe that if they reveal the truth about their financial attitudes (say, that they avoid money matters and are afraid of dealing with money), they won't merit any respect. Some cringe at the thought of baring their souls about money because their own parents fought a great deal over finance and they don't wish to open this particular can of worms. And some hold fast to the belief that their attitude is *ipso facto* the *correct* attitude—and no discussion or explanation is necessary.

If any of these reflect your fiancé's position, do not be discouraged. *You* take the first step and own up to your feelings about money. Find a time when you both are free to take a breather and when it is not imperative that you make a quick decision about, say, whether or not to pop for the engraved lettering. Then share with your partner what you think money represents to you on an emotional level (security, self-esteem, independence?) and how it was discussed and dealt with in your family. Confide any thoughts and feelings about money, even those you fear are irrational ("We'll end up in the poor-house, I just know it!"). Confide your plans and goals (if you're a schemer) or your fantasies (if you're a dreamer). Then allow your partner to respond to what you said and share his own feelings on the subject—without criticism or, for that matter, interruption of any sort.

Next, take turns expressing what it is you fear most about each other's attitude, and what is it you admire most about that attitude. Don't neglect the admiration aspect, as it is crucial in helping you to keep from polarizing too much. Finally, ask each other if there's any other issue you've been avoiding while you focus relentlessly on monetary concerns. If you're honest, you may each learn that the other is, say, fearful of giving in too much (which they've been expressing by not *giving* so much when it comes to money) or fearful of losing the relationship (which they've been expressing as a fear of losing their money).

Now that you are effectively communicating, you are much better equipped to tackle specific issues relating to your wedding expenses. Go forth and employ some of the other skills you've already learned about. *Prioritize.* Find out what is most important to whom. Then compromise. After your talks about personal money attitudes, you are operating from a better vantage point. You know what it takes to push your partner's money buttons—so try not to do so! If capitulating about a certain expenditure will keep him from experiencing paroxysms of anxiety ("If we add one more hot hors d'oeuvre to the buffet, we'll bounce a check to the caterer and spend our honeymoon in the county jail"), so be it. Cancel those roasted-Brie balls. You'll survive.

While you're at it, don't forget to *delegate.* As we already know, there are umpteen reasons why your families may not be able to go "by the book" when it comes to contributing funds for your wedding. But if either family is interested in helping, and able to do so, discuss with your fiancé what it would mean to each of you to accept that help.

If either of you feels there are too many emotional strings attached ("When my mother pays, my mother takes charge!"), you may decide to say a sincere thank-you and decline. But if you can accept with equanimity the well-meant offer of assistance in any given area, great! What's more, you may even wish to delegate the negotiating process for a certain expense over to those who are paying for it. (If your father is springing for transportation, perhaps he would be willing to discuss with the head of Ralph's Limo Service why his drivers get triple overtime for working on Sundays.)

THE BOTTOM LINE

Naturally prioritization and delegation can only be done within the context of an overall umbrella sum you and your mate have agreed to spend for your nuptials. Like other things, if this sum is in dispute, that dispute is best reconciled *after* a conversation that allows room to vent money attitudes, fantasies, and fears.

For knowing these will help you understand the internal emotional pressures each of you is dealing with in making your suggestion for a suitable amount. In addition, you and your partner may wish to share your feelings about the *external* social pressure that factors in to this decision.

As of this book's writing, the average cost of a wedding in America is about $19,000.[1] And with big weddings back in fashion, that number is unlikely to decrease anytime soon. But does that mean that if you spend less, your wedding is somehow below average?

Naturally the answer is no. Sure, you would like everyone you invite to have a good time, but this does not mean you should mortgage your future to make some sort of impression. There are countless ways to host a day of merrymaking that do not require declaring bankruptcy before you even embark on the journey of married life. If spending a great deal of money is either beyond your actual means or simply not something you care to do, prepare to get resourceful and flexible.

There are all sorts of strategies you may use to cut wedding costs, from bargaining with merchants (haggling is very fashionable in the nineties) to hunting down low-cost alternatives to traditional wedding sites and services (do you want to marry in a botanical garden, or have a friend with culinary expertise handle the catering?). Timing can also be important. You might consider a wedding brunch instead of a dinner. And you might wish to steer clear of the "high wedding season" (May through October), when prices tend to be at their peak.

But perhaps the best strategy of all for someone bogged down with the emotional weight of Pre-Marital Syndrome is to let your *personal creativity* come forth.

By now you may have heard of the concept of "flow," a peaceful and contented mental state people find themselves in when they are absorbed in an activity that is stimulating and challenging (the challenge being suited to their own level of skill). A determined tennis player wholly focused on his backstroke, a nurturing gardener contentedly planting her bulbs, an opera singer trilling in mid-aria are all examples of people who might well be experiencing this transcendent state. What does the state transcend? *Self-consciousness!* The more engrossed you are in a pleasurable task that you are good at, the less apt you are to be anxious about the things that usually occupy your churning mind.

So, consider doing something personal for your wedding that will not only save you money but give you pleasure. I know a couple (an artist and a photographer) who designed and made their own wedding invitations (reproductions of clocks that announced the time and date of the event). I also know a would-be chef who invented her own wedding-cake recipe after many happy hours of experimenting (a half cup of Grand Marnier made all the difference, she reported). But don't get the wrong impression. You don't have to be Martha Stewart or Betty Crocker to get into the spirit of wedding creativity. You might simply choose to shop creatively for bridesmaids' gifts (that don't cost a fortune but clearly bear the mark of your personal touch) or hunt down a festive, off-the-beaten-track ethnic restaurant for a rehearsal supper.

The point is to have some fun with your wedding planning and take your mind off your worries while practicing some sensible frugality at the same time. If you are a Righteous Romantic, your creative "flow" may well give you a much-needed respite from your search to purchase perfection. If you're a Teary Tester, it will distract you from the wrong-headed notion that your wedding expenditures equal the amount of love in your relationship. And if you're a Halfway Hysteric, it will actually give you a nice sense of balance and stability—for a change!

THE COST OF IGNORING MONEY MATTERS

All in all, when it comes to money and weddings, there are two kinds of costs one must consider. The first is the literal cost. Will you spend $19,000, $9,000, $90,000? That of course depends on what you have, what you want, and what you may be willing to sacrifice. Only you and your fiancé can figure the bottom line.

But there may lurk a hidden cost, unless you are careful. That is the toll money matters will take on your relationship unless you become aware of hidden emotional agendas that may surround money for both you and your mate—and mutually begin to divulge them.

This can be a daunting undertaking, to be sure. But by this point in your march to the altar, you should be getting used to dealing with these Back-Burnered issues. Again, don't discount your fear. Acknowledge it. But search for the fallacy that could be fueling it and the reality that can set you free.

FEAR: "Since we've started talking about money, it's clear we'll never agree on it. We're hopelessly different. We're doomed."

FALLACY: You're assuming that other couples surely aren't this extreme in their opposing views. Or that if they are, they either get divorced or have miserable marriages. Wrong!

REALITY: Money misunderstandings may in fact lead to serious marital discontent. But the misunderstandings don't result so much from a couple's differing attitudes (remember, even if you start out similar, you're likely to polarize) as they do from not acknowledging and sharing the sources of one's own attitudes and not allowing room for one's partner to do the same.

REMEDY: As you prepare for your wedding, you

are in the infant stages of a relationship you hope will grow very, very old. In tackling money matters related to your wedding you may falter and fumble, as any infant does when learning to grapple with the world around him. But you need to maneuver through this awkward stage in order to go on. So, even if you can't successfully resolve all your disputes around money and your wedding with such skills as prioritization, compromise, and delegation, don't give up on communication. And if your partner isn't yet willing to communicate openly about his relationship with money, show some patience.

Meanwhile, continue to work on understanding your own relationship to money. For chances are, you will see that it is more complicated than you thought.

CHAPTER FIVE

TWICE-TOLD JOKES
AND VANISHING
TABLE MANNERS

*Keep your eyes wide open before marriage,
and half shut afterwards.*

— *BEN FRANKLIN*

The preceding two chapters may have given you the impression that the vast majority of your engagement will be spent being agitated about wedding matters—stylistic, financial, and otherwise. Not true at all! If you are like most brides-to-be, you may rest assured that you will spend a goodly portion of your time being irritated about other things as well.

In our discussion of money it was noted that during the dating stage of most relationships, people tend to be on best behavior when it comes to fiscal demeanor. But what about other sorts of demeanor? Interestingly the interpersonal dynamics of a relationship begin to shift in subtle but significant ways once the prospect of permanence has been broached.

Do you have the feeling your fiancé is taking you for granted? Does he seem somewhat less attentive, a tad (or a scad) less considerate? Has his passion become more passive? Has his chivalry quotient deteriorated appreciably? And do you definitely not appreciate it?

WHEN YOUR SUITOR GETS SETTLED

Well, you are not the first woman to take umbrage at a husband-to-be's "diminishing returns." Far from it. Nearly every woman I've ever queried about this subject has admitted to a certain amount of annoyance as her partner undergoes the transition from the suitor state to the settled state. For example:

• "My boyfriend brought me roses all the time when we were dating, and when he was out of town on business, he'd send them FTD. Once we got engaged, the flowers stopped arriving. Not right away, but gradually. I didn't mind at first, since we were supposed to be saving money, and I thought he was just being practical. But the bouquets kept getting fewer and farther between. After a few months with not a blossom in sight, I started thinking, 'Hey, what's really going on? Don't I rate a few *buds* at least?'"

• "This may sound ridiculous, I know, but after my boyfriend became my fiancé, he started to relax about his table manners. One night we'd had take-out pizza, and after a few slices he let out the biggest belch I'd ever heard in the middle of our conversation and didn't even say, 'Excuse me.' Now, I don't mean to sound prissy or anything, but the fact is I had never heard him do this before, ever. Later on it got even worse. He came over to kiss me, and I realized he'd ordered extra garlic on his half of the pizza. I'm not a garlic fan, as he knew, but when I wrinkled my nose and complained, he just said, 'Hey, you're stuck with me now, honey. You might as well get used to it.' I had visions of myself being chained to this huge bulb of garlic for all eternity, like Prometheus to a rock."

• "One of the things that attracted me to my boyfriend was that he was such a dazzling conversationalist. When we were courting, he always had some wonderful, amusing anecdote to tell. Until we got engaged. Then I noticed something. We'd go out to dinner with different friends of mine who wanted to meet him and he'd tell the same story to each one. They loved it, of course, since they'd never heard it before, but was I supposed to spend my whole life laughing about his wrong-way touchdown on the eighth-grade football team? To make matters worse, when we were alone together, it seemed like he had less to say than ever. Right after we got engaged, in fact, he suggested one night we watch the news on TV while eating dinner. After that it became a habit. So much for scintillating repartee."

• "Not long after our engagement my fiancé did something I thought was really inconsiderate. We went off for a weekend retreat with other members of his law firm, which was an annual summer ritual. On Friday night I overheard my husband-to-be trying to set up a tennis game for Saturday morning between himself and his boss. His boss was tempted, but said his wife might not be pleased with this arrangement as she wouldn't have anything to occupy her. Whereupon my fiancé volunteered me to drive his wife to a nearby outlet mall for some shopping. Now, I don't like my husband's boss's wife. And I don't like outlet malls. I like *tennis* and had expected to get on the courts myself, as my boyfriend well knew. Yet here he was making promises on my behalf!"

If it feels to you like your tales of premarital woe might fit in nicely with this chorus of complaint, welcome to the club: the Reality and Readjustment Club, that is. The sampling you've just heard is typical of some of the pitfalls of long-term commitment. Like it or not, familiarization and habituation do alter the nature of romantic relationships. The question is, how are you going to react?

A Righteous Romantic can really find herself in a bind when signs of habituation set in. Should her partner's behavior fail to live up to her prescribed image of what it ought to be, her *modus operandi* is to pretend not to notice—especially when other people are around. But beneath the pretense of perfection she persists in maintaining, she will likely be seething. She may be readying to blow her stack in a serious way—after the wedding. Meanwhile she may give her husband-to-be a frosty dose of the silent treatment.

A Teary Tester, you won't be surprised to learn, will likely greet each new transgression of romantic etiquette with a fresh cascade. Every day she's adding more evidence to her case for running off and joining the French Foreign Legion. Anything strikes her as preferable to hooking up with this . . . *beast*. And she's not ashamed to let anyone know it. Indeed, she lets everyone know it at least once a day.

As for the Halfway Hysteric, she'll generally flip-flop from one mode to the other. One day it will be tight-lipped denial—even if it nearly kills her to bite her tongue. The next day it will be floods of lamentations. And with every perceived slight her mood swings may grow a little more extreme.

Perhaps you would like to avail yourself of a different, more constructive sort of reaction than these. This is not a bad idea. Indeed, not all members of the Reality and Readjustment Club need to put themselves through such emotional contortions. Readjustment is required, all right, but it goes easier if you come to grips with reality first.

JUST THE FACTS, MA'AM

Not too long from now you will be taking wedding vows that include promises to "love and honor" your husband "for richer, for poorer," and "in sickness and in health." Those are lovely—and deeply meaningful—sentiments. However, if those vows were also to include some of the less lofty and more practical aspects of married life, they might say something like, "Out of love and respect for you and for our relationship I will do my best to tolerate your twice-told jokes and vanishing table manners, your unintentional but aggravating forgetfulness, your complacency and occasional presumptuousness, your fleeting flatulence, and those grunts that you so often seem to substitute for meaningful discourse."

Because the fact is you will have to tolerate all those things in your spouse—*just as he will have to tolerate identical or equivalent irritating characteristics in you.*

Even now, in your marital prelude, you can begin to see that inevitable changes are weaving their way into the fabric of your liaison. And certain trade-offs are taking place.

Though poets and philosophers have long waxed eloquent on the mysterious and mystical aspects of romantic love, modern researchers of a more scientific bent have tried to break love down into various analyzable components. One such researcher, psychologist Robert Sternberg of Yale University, has isolated what he sees as three key components in the romantic equation: passion, intimacy, and commitment. The ascendance and decline of these three elements, he says, follow distinct courses over time.[1]

Passion—excitedly amorous and erotic emotions—is what fuels a typical relationship at its inception. Chances are, passion is what magnetized you and your fiancé in the first place. It sparked your physical ardor, to be sure. And it also kindled something more abstract: your initial starry-eyed appraisal of your beau as Mr. Wonderful. For in the grips of passion you tend to view the object of your affections as a flawless diamond—precious, perfect, and rare.

Intimacy, the second component of what we call love, is a sense of affinity, camaraderie, and mutual understanding. It has to do with talking, tickling, whispering, winking, and feeling easy in each other's company. While it doesn't hit you like a ton of bricks, as does passion, it grows on you, gradually but inveterately.

Intimacy, though, is a funny thing. Sometimes, even as it is expanding, it seems to be dormant. You don't notice, perhaps, after the initial stages of a relationship, that you're growing closer all the time. Instead you may notice that the amount of time you spend trading stories about your childhood and sharing your hopes and dreams for the future is *diminishing,* while you spend more and more time fielding conversational gambits such as "Have you seen my socks?" and "You *know* I hate tofu."

What gives? Increasing intimacy, believe it or not!

Studies have shown that intense expressions of emotion thrive on *uncertainty* and *interruption.* When a couple makes a promise to marry, they are, in effect, agreeing to do away with such barriers to togetherness. Nevertheless there comes a point in an acknowledged long-term relationship where conspicuous intimacy is replaced by a more subtle and inconspicuous, though in some ways more stable, sort.

In one of those aforementioned trade-offs, couples in evolving relationships swap intense initial intimacy for everyday intimacy-in-action. For indeed you can only regale each other with your personal history, grand plans, fondest dreams, and theories of the birth of the universe so much before certain nuts-and-bolts considerations come creeping back into your consciousness.

Where *are* those socks anyway? He assumes you know, because you know his habits so well. (Ergo, you know he left them in the laundry bag—as usual.) What *about* that tofu? He's miffed that you tried to sneak it into the lasagna—again. (But you're watching his cholesterol and there's this ongoing struggle over his dairy quota.)

So you pretend you don't know where his socks are—just for a laugh—until he gets desperate. So he pouts about the cholesterol and sneaks a cheeseburger—and you catch him. You rib each other, you rile each other, you shake your heads and smile, or pout and sigh.

This is intimacy-in-action. It presupposes an established closeness that by and large goes unquestioned. It bypasses formalities. Its scope includes not just life's epiphanies but its trivialities. For unless you share the little things—even the mundane things—it's difficult to share the big ones.

Which brings us to the third aspect of love's equation: commitment. The very essence of the commitment component is a sense of shared responsibility. There's both an expectation and an obligation to stay on board for a lifelong journey (without uncertainty, without interruption) regardless of bumps in the road.

But now we come to the matter of trade-offs again. As the commitment between two partners grows, the intimacy tends to grow—even as the nature of that intimacy changes. The raw passion, however, tends to *wane* over time. Quick to ignite (almost instantaneous in some cases) and swift to heat, it is, alas, relatively quick to cool. And as burning passion fades, so do its outward manifestations.

The bouquets and cards and trinkets don't show up as often. Neither do those ardent declarations of undying adoration you may have heard daily at your relationship's dawn. Perhaps most significant of all—and most potentially dangerous to a marriage in the making—partners no longer in the grips of full-blown passion do not tend to view each other as the crowning achievement of Creation here on earth. Indeed, your mate can, rather abruptly, begin to seem somewhat the worse for the wear. In place of rose-colored spectacles is a magnifying glass that actually seems to amplify your partner's peccadilloes.

Now, combine this dilution of passion and idealization with the shift in the nature of intimacy and what have you got?

Probably vexation. ("I can't believe he's acting this way!")

Possibly indignation. ("Harrumph! I can't believe he's doing this *to me*.")

And potentially boredom.

ARE WE IN ENNUI?

Right now, in your betrothed state, with passion, intimacy, and commitment in flux, the potential for ennui is yet another dilemma with which you will have to contend. Chances are your fiancé's relatively unceremonious behavior toward you is being supplemented by his lessening need and desire to impress and entertain you. After all, he's beginning to think of the two of you as a unit. You're not someone on whom he has to practice high-gear wooing any longer, and he knows he doesn't have to impress you to win you. For you and he have reached a comfortable plateau together.

But perhaps *you* are used to a different outcome in your relationships. If you are like many contemporary women, you have enjoyed the attentions of several other boyfriends before deciding to marry. You may have been the one to "love and lose" or you may have been the one to terminate those prior relationships. But either way, if you have had a series of beaus, it's likely you've not had as many plateaus as you have had highs and lows.

You got together and hit it off: a peak. You started to see each other more and more: a higher peak. Things got rocky: a downward slope. You broke up: a valley.

After enough of these you start to get used to the rhythm of love's comings and goings. The highs are a thrill, the lows a dramatic spill. But they're both exciting—and it's not uncommon to become acclimated to that *level* of excitement, be the circumstance positive or negative.

Now, however, as a bride-to-be, you face the prospect of permanence with someone. The same someone. Forevermore. And at this delicate prenuptial stage of the game, that may seem to you like you're stuck in the wide, flat plains of Kansas—with nary a peak or valley in sight.

You may start to get nervous. A part of you wonders, "Is this all there is?" And out of that nervousness, you may weep or withdraw or pick fights or—cancel the caterer. But the nagging sensation, which is underneath these diversions, won't go away.

But *is this all there is?*

Happily the answer is no.

Monotony and malaise, vexation and indignation need not ruin your engaged nor your wedded fate—so long as you realize that neither is it your fate to be dazzled, delighted, and endlessly entertained by your husband-to-be for the rest of your days. And so long as you are willing to develop coping mechanisms to help you assimilate the natural fluctuations of passion, intimacy, and commitment.

READJUSTMENTS

As therapists have observed, and as studies of the dynamics of couples have borne out, the prime cause of boredom and many related problems in long-term relationships is the inability or unwillingness of partners to make the transition from one stage to the next.

You are, even as you read these words, smack bang in the middle of a crucial initial transition. But with all that's going on, it's hard to see the forest for the trees.

You see passion fading and think—mistakenly—that it's evaporating. You see intimacy evolving, and think—wrongly—that it's vanishing. You see commitment deepening and you grow frightened. For you suspect—quite rightly—that commitment standing alone without love's two other key elements is essentially a ball and chain.

You need some help in assimilating what's really happening.

In the epigraph to this chapter the sagacious Ben Franklin advises, "Keep your eyes wide open before marriage, and half shut afterwards." By this, one presumes he meant you should choose your mate wisely and then accept your choice (with all his inevitable, all-too-human shortcomings) with grace.

Good counsel, this.

But you are in a funny kind of situation. You've made your choice but haven't formalized it. There's still time to exit—perhaps not gracefully, certainly not without pain—but with relative expeditiousness compared with what it takes to dissolve a marriage. You're not yet predisposed to the benign postmarital acceptance mode of Golden Anniversary celebrants who charmingly shrug and say, "He drove me crazy. So I learned to live with it." On the other hand, keeping your eyes peeled for your partner's transgressions is probably no fun—for either of you.

For you, then, a middle course between eternal vigilance and the relaxed "that's the way it is" approach of a veteran seems called for. This engagement interim is the ideal time to start practicing strategies aimed at keeping passion's pilot light aglow even as intimacy's strange, changing winds may cause the flame to flicker.

With the goal of steering the middle course in mind, here are some suggestions:

SET LIMITS ON WHAT'S ACCEPTABLE

In many ways it's absolutely wonderful that your fiancé feels more comfortable and relaxed around you than ever before. After all, if you can't let your hair down around your lifemate, with whom can you? To some extent, it may be a relief to both of you to forgo certain formalities. After all, it's a marriage you're putting together here, not a diplomatic corps. But even bearing this in mind, there may come a point where for you enough is enough. When does a healthy lack of ostentatiousness cross the line into downright offensiveness? It's a very individual matter. Thus the only "correct" answer can be: When you think so.

If you're bent out of shape about dodging those swinging

doors that your fiancé has stopped holding open for you, you have every right to speak up and spare yourself a bloody nose. Likewise you may choose to vocalize your objections if your spouse develops a postbetrothal habit of barging in on you while you're in the bathroom. ("Hey, what have you got to hide?" he asks jovially.) But even if his infractions are more along the lines of etiquette misdemeanors than felonies (say he chugs orange juice from the carton or leaves used dental floss in the sink), you are entitled to speak your piece if you feel that certain sensibilities that are important to you are being snubbed.

There is nothing wrong with setting limits, so long as you do so with affection and good humor. In general, a gambit like, "I know this isn't Buckingham Palace, but how about a *little* decorum?" will get you a lot farther than, "What barn were *you* raised in?"

Also, be sure to air your grievances in private rather than in front of bemused onlookers. As you already know, "public opinion" regarding the wisdom of your choice of husband may be mixed due to deep-seated separation anxieties among your friends and family. Why provide them with ammunition to feed their fears?

ACKNOWLEDGE YOUR OWN ACTIONS

Before you go compiling and airing a laundry list of complaints, however, be advised that postengagement lapses are usually a two-way street. Is there any behavior of yours that may be causing your mate to wince? Think about it.

Wasn't it just the other night that you wordlessly seized the remote control to hunt down *Murphy Brown* just as he was hunkering down for an evening of NCAA finals? Wasn't it a few weeks back that you committed him—without benefit of consultation—to spending an evening at your Cousin Miriam's chamber-music recital (never mind that he hates chamber music almost as much as he loathes Cousin Miriam)?

There's no great shame or blame in your doing things of this nature of course. Just know that you *have* done them and let that knowledge serve to temper your own protests.

And don't neglect to consider where the two of you seem to have made tacit agreements renouncing some of the formalities of courtship. Isn't it you, as well as your mate, who has stopped pretending you *always* eat fried chicken with a knife and fork? And isn't it you, as well as he, who has forgone playing "dress up" for quiet evenings at home and taken to hanging out in sneakers and sweat pants? You can't reasonably expect your partner to uphold a standard of behavior you yourself no longer subscribe to.

CREATE SURPRISES

With familiarization and habituation encroaching on your passion, you may well feel like you are getting into a rut. There are fewer surprises, many engaged women complain, and less spontaneity. So what's stopping you from creating some!?

Why not:

• Leave a series of clever love notes for your fiancé to discover?

• Buy him a stuffed animal or silly T-shirt or other suitably playful, goofy gift?

• Sign the two of you up for dance lessons, or sailing lessons, or Bungie Jumping 101—any untried activity that holds some appeal for both of you and that you can sample and master together?

And because engagement periods, with their shifting love components—and of course the emotional drains of wedding planning—can sometimes induce a case of the sexual ho-hums, why not:

• Put on a Johnny Mathis record and tell him you want to "make out"?

• Have him help you pick out something scandalously sexy from one of those X-rated lingerie catalogues?

• Hold a moratorium on wedding planning and instead plan a trip to somewhere charming (you get a fireplace instead of free HBO) and remote (no fax)? Take charge of this yourself and keep the details a closely guarded secret. Make sure your boyfriend saves the dates but don't tell him anything about the itinerary until you're en route.

The point is that all relationships need rejuvenation from time to time, even those that aren't very old yet. So, don't sit around waiting to *react* to your mate's action. Instead take a *proactive* role—and make something happen.

USE POSITIVE REINFORCEMENT

Speaking of reactions, when your partner does something you like, for example, something considerate (he offers you the first slice of pizza—the one *without* the garlic and *with* most of the pepperoni), something gallant (he asks Cousin Miriam to dance at a family function), or something downright silly and adorable (*what's* that he's wearing on his head?), let him know you're delighted.

Simply saying, "I love it when you do that" or "What a sweetheart," or, depending on your personal style, "That really lights my burners," goes a long way toward getting your man to *do it again*.

DON'T TALK TOO MUCH ABOUT TALKING TOO LITTLE

By the time you are several months into your engagement, you may be very frustrated indeed about the quantity and quality of your mutual conversation. This book has already mentioned several instances where it would be a good idea for you and your fiancé to talk about expectations and anxieties, priorities and concerns. It's also pointed out that you need to listen to your partner's point of view in addition to advancing your own.

But what if there comes a point where even if you're ready and willing to listen and you put your antennae up, all you receive is a faint hum? While you scan the airwaves for "meaningful contact," all your fiancé seems to be emitting is the dull background noise of daily business ("Have you been using my razor again?" "*How* long does it take to boil rice?"), interspersed with an occasional news or sports bulletin ("Darn that Congress" "Damn those Mets"). And even though you are now aware this is a new phase of intimacy, you can't believe this ought to constitute the whole of your discourse.

Well, it oughtn't to. But heart-to-heart talks oughtn't to be the whole of it either. While heart-to-hearts are important, it's best not to attempt to have them every day and not to dissect every aspect of your relationship. A certain amount of "down time" from heavy topics is healthy, normal, and desirable. When you would like to have a serious talk, however, you will greatly aid and abet your own cause by creating an opening in a relaxed, nonpressuring manner.

Don't put your fiancé on the defensive by haranguing him with accusations that *we never talk*. Don't say, "We have to talk," as if you are Chicken Little and you've just found out the sky is falling. And don't introduce every topic of discussion as if it's a life-or-death imperative.

In general, men are not as gung ho as women when it comes to talking about relationships. They like to be in the flow of a relationship rather than scrutinize it. Women are not born with a "share your feelings" gene, but they *are* socially reinforced for being more forthcoming about emotions. Hence your man may be able to learn something from you in that area. But you should be able to learn something from him also, which is that it's often okay just to relax and enjoy.

ARE YOU TURNING INTO YOUR MARRIED FRIENDS?

Near the start of this book it was suggested that one of the first "spoiler" thoughts that generally flit through the mind of an engaged woman is the discouraging idea that she and her mate will somehow go from a dynamic duo to stuck-in-the-mud fuddy-duddies. With passion, intimacy, and commitment in flux, you may indeed be picturing yourself down the road, fossilized together, preserved in glass, with a crowd of still-single onlookers pointing at you and commenting, "Ah, yes, those certainly *look* like married people. See that glazed expression in their eyes?"

But when you conjure that fatal vision, consider the following fear that was confided to me from a young woman on the verge of marriage. And consider the advice she was given:

FEAR: "My married friends' lives seem so dull compared with the single life. Last night I called Janice at nine P.M. and she said the phone woke up her husband. I don't know if I can live like that. Will I still love my husband when *he* falls asleep at nine o'clock?"

FALLACY: Marriage should be endlessly "exciting."

REALITY: There is an ancient Chinese curse that says, "May you live in interesting times." An equivalent modern hex might be, "May your marriage be endlessly exciting." One of the greatest pleasures of genuine loving camaraderie and companionship is the simple joy of sharing "down time."

REMEDY: It's time for an honest chat with those married friends of yours. Ask them what aspects of their everyday life together they like best. Chances are they'll say it's the snuggling, the private jokes, the nights when they get to rent a video, screen phone calls, and share Egg Foo Yung straight out of the carton. If they maintain they're never happy unless they're attending a formal dinner party for twelve, chances are the party will end sooner than they think.

CHAPTER SIX

FAMILY MATTERS,
PRESENT TENSE
("*I'M* RELATED TO *THEM*?")

In my very own self, I am a part of my family.
— D. H. LAWRENCE

*Nobody who has not been in the interior of a family can say
what the difficulties of any individual of that family may be.*
— JANE AUSTEN

Now you have some methods for dealing with your fiancé's
eccentricities and idiosyncrasies, his little flaws and annoying
faux pas. Your repertoire of coping mechanisms has expanded.
But chances are, that repertoire will still need enlarging. For in
getting engaged you are linking your life not merely to that of
another imperfect and frustrating human being but to many
such paragons of imperfection—who are soon to be your
relations.

Ah, it was so simple while you were just dating. It was you
and him. Him and you. Perhaps there was an occasional get-
together with another couple, but you mostly spent such evenings gazing lovestruck at one another and ignoring them
anyhow.

Now he wants you to get to know—and love—his folks,
his siblings, his great-grandpa, his third cousins and his
brother-in-law's mom and dad. Congratulations! You've taken

on an entourage, and they all want to get together to watch Monday-night Rams games. At your place.

But it's no problem. Or so he says. If you're bored, you can go out for a bite instead—with his sister-in-law, who wants to get to know you better so that she can sign you up to peddle her new line of homemade skin care products in your spare time.

Okay, okay. So these folks may not be exactly what you'd pictured. And perhaps you are not as enthused about being in their company as your fiancé would like. But maybe you should just bite your tongue until after the wedding. After all, you don't want to insult anyone—yet. On the other hand, maybe you should speak up now. These Rams fans are spilling suds on your rug. Your ingratiating sister-in-law has appeared, brandishing a sample case of Miracle Moisturizing Mist. How much more can you stand?

The truth is it's hard to know just what to do when the man you love wants to share you with his nearest and dearest. Part of you may be flattered and eager to fit in. Part of you thinks, "Who *are* these people and what are they doing in my life?" And yet *another* part of you knows that you must manage your natural ambivalence wisely and well, for these people are bound to impact your life and your marriage—whether you like it or not.

There's no question that the more a couple's relationship extends to accommodate people outside the twosome, the more complicated matters may become. In the engaged state the introduction of the "family factor" into your love equation can definitely be unnerving. For if your spouse-to-be's family does not behave "appropriately," or go along with your way of thinking, or treat you just the way you prefer to be treated, or in any other way fail to live up to your expectations, that may give you second thoughts about the entire undertaking of wedlock.

An inordinate number of married women seem to be able

to recall in lurid detail moments in the course of their betrothal when a member of their husband's family did something so preposterous or offensive as to instill in them serious doubts concerning the viability of ever marrying into their clan. Among the incidents that will live in infamy in the chronicles of Premarital Syndrome:

> The Day My Fiancé's Parents Showed Up at My Parents' Country Club in Sweat Suits ("I could have died.")
>
> The Rehearsal Dinner When His Father Left His Wallet Home ("Yeah, right. What a *skinflint*.")
>
> The Way His Family Tried to Make Us Serve Macrobiotic Food at the Wedding ("Ugh!")
>
> The Time His Mother Said *My* Mother Should Diet ("The nerve.")
>
> The Time I Heard His Family Whispering That I Wore My Skirts Too Short ("What gall.")

While these specific obstacles to familial bliss may not lie in your particular path, you certainly get the idea. At some point along the way to your wedding you may be deeply disappointed or utterly put out by various things your fiancé's kin do or don't do. So what will *you* do?

If you're a classic Righteous Romantic, you will experience inevitable disillusionment as your family-to-be threatens to burst your precarious bubble of bliss. Once you face the realization that the new family you're supposed to embrace does not combine the warmth of the Waltons, the wealth of the Windsors, and the charisma of the Kennedys, you'll be faced with a fit of what psychologists call cognitive dissonance. You'll futilely attempt to reconcile two ideas that don't mesh—that is, the perfect wedding and perfect marriage with the fact that your parents-in-law are "defective." As usual, it's "happily ever after" you're after, but how are you supposed to find this panacea marrying into a bunch of people prone to dining out in leisurewear?

If you're a Teary Tester, coping with your beau's family could provide all sorts of occasions for histrionics. Suppose that infuriating mate of yours refuses to stand up to that parsnip-pushing macrobiotic mother of his, leaving you to tangle with her while he begs off. *Wah!* Worse yet, suppose he actively takes her side and agrees that your wedding reception ought to be a wheat-free, dairy-free, sugar-free affair (pointing out, to boot, that your family of pasta-loving pastry gorgers could stand to shape up a bit). *Double wah!!* Since, as a Teary Tester, you are hypersensitive to any hint that your mate does not hold your preferences dear (therefore he doesn't love you, never loved you, et cetera), you will be quick to view any disagreement in which he favors his kin as a display of his rampant disloyalty.

If you are a Halfway Hysteric, you will have yet more opportunities to vacillate. At certain points you might idealize your future in-laws and yearn for their approval and acceptance. But should you sense they *dis*approve of you (citing your preference for miniskirts or any other reason), you can quickly switch gears and cheerfully imagine them embarking on a one-way journey to a parallel universe.

None of these tactics, however, are apt to pave the way toward the kind of familial harmony that would stand to benefit your relationship. Clearly, at this point you need to begin to master the art and science of integrating your husband's clan into your world and vice versa. To do so, you need to understand what makes your new family tick. You also need to balance your own desire for approval and fear of rejection with your rights to set limits in certain crucial areas.

FIELDWORK

The first thing you ought to be aware of is that virtually every family comprises a kind of distinct civilization, with its own habits and customs. So, as you get to know your fiancé's family, do not be unduly surprised if you find they manifest certain daily divergences from your own. Perhaps:

• They eat the salad course at the end of the meal, not before
• They take turns clearing the table (In your house Mother always did it)
• They set the thermostat ten degrees cooler than you're used to
• They root for the "wrong" baseball team

Each family also has its own rules and values. Don't be surprised, then, if they seem to have different ideas about what's important and what's insignificant, what's perceived as special and what's taken for granted, what's permissible and what's looked upon askance. Suppose:

• They are adamant that Christmas gifts should not be opened until Christmas morning (You always did it Christmas Eve)
• They laugh at knock-knock jokes (but never the off-color kind your brothers favor)
• They've all hiked the Appalachian Trail and know how to pitch and make fires by rubbing two twigs together (Your family's idea of roughing it on holiday is to forgo room service and sample the breakfast buffet)

As you can see, there is a great deal to learn about any family, and a great deal to get used to. The best way to broach the dilemma of meeting and contending with your future in-laws is to consider yourself an anthropologist on a field trip to an alien culture. Like any good field researcher you ought not to try to enter an unknown situation with a goal of *changing* it. Your mission should be to observe it, understand it, and learn what's expected of you as you ease your way into the system.

As a newcomer to your fiancé's family, it does not do for

you to challenge long-standing practices and traditions. What good will it do you, after all, to exclaim, "*What,* you're eating salad *now?*" or to insist, "I want my Christmas presents to-night." You probably won't get them to do things your way, and even if you do, you're still placing an emotional wedge between you that will be hard to dislodge.

As of now, your job is to try to learn this family's ground rules, strange though they may seem to you. It's also a time to learn what they want from you and see if it's possible to comply. If what they want is something you can deal with, acquiescence is in order. It won't kill you to chuckle at a knock-knock joke that you don't find amusing. And taking a turn clearing the table will stand you in good stead. Of course, if your in-laws want your participation in something you really don't feel comfortable with, you must employ yet another new skill—*declining without deriding.*

Suppose this indefatigable group of Appalachian Trail backpackers wants you to come along for a two-week jaunt in the Adirondacks. You'd rather have root canal than face poison ivy and snakes, sleep on the cold ground, and tend to your personal-hygiene needs behind a mulberry bush. Fine, but you needn't run through your litany of dreads and try to convince them to sign up for two weeks at Club Med ("for a *real* vacation"). Instead try to say something complimentary about their undertaking and about them. ("It sounds so adventurous. What a brave bunch you are.") Then help them hear that though you are unable to do as they wish, it is for reasons that have nothing to do with them, but with you. ("I'm not really the outdoors type, and I'm afraid I'd slow you all down.") Finally be sure to wish them well.

Here you are still behaving like an anthropologist, for you are careful not to devalue the things that this family holds dear. But now there's something else you must learn. For there is an aspect of their civilization that most families hold dearest of all.

WHAT'S THEIR STORY?

Every family, like every culture that ever existed, has its own set of self-definitions. That is to say, they have deeply ingrained beliefs about what they themselves are like as a group and how they are perceived by others. These beliefs form the "stories" of their world. For example:

- We're a casual, carefree, fun-loving bunch
- We're pillars of respectability
- We're in tip-top condition and will all live to be a hundred
- We always get along and never raise our voices

In addition to these self-assigned group identities, families also tend to assign labels and roles to each of their members. And everyone in this civilization-in-miniature tacitly agrees not only to play his or her part but to behave in ways that reinforce the roles of the others. For instance:

- Dad's a genius, but very forgetful (and we all laugh it off and call him the Absentminded Professor)
- Aunt Louise drinks too much sherry (but we all pretend not to notice)

Often the individual labels and group identities fit together hand in glove, for example:

- Mom's the frail, nervous type and can't be upset (and *that's why* we never raise our voices).

Whatever you do at this delicate stage of your relationship with your fiancé's family, be sure you don't challenge their stories—for they are nothing less than the *foundation* of their civilization. Instead, you must set yourself the task of taking the stories in and gleaning their various nuances.

Learning about this crucial aspect of your new clan can be somewhat more complex than simply noticing their customs, habits, likes, and dislikes. For these stories are not going to be "told" to you per se. Rare indeed are the in-laws who will sit you down and say, "Hello there, dear. We see ourselves as very respectable people." Or, "Welcome to the family. We all get along like peas in a pod, don't you think?" Indeed, a family is likely not even to be consciously aware that they jointly subscribe to a "story" about themselves and portray themselves according to their self-definitions. So you will have to allow some time to discern what image it is that your new family likes to put forth to the world.

What's more, family stories are not necessarily even objectively accurate. Maybe the family that believes it's so close doesn't get along as well as they think. Perhaps the "ultra-respectable" ones have a black sheep or two in their midst (Aunt Louise, the sherry sampler, for instance). It can be very tempting to point out the discrepancies in their "stories." But the wise bride-to-be won't give in to any such temptation.

Accurate or not, you will have to respect the self-defining beliefs that are woven through the cloth of your new family. And you will have to be sensitive to their consequences, because you will have to deal with those consequences now and for many years to come.

Until you allow yourself to be educated about the family stories of your betrothed's clan, you are at a disadvantage— and at dangerous risk of having your Pre-Marital Syndrome stress escalate. For you may be taking offense at things that really have little to do with you.

Take for example, the Rehearsal Dinner When His Father Left His Wallet Home. What the bride-to-be in this case did not know was that her fiancé's family had bestowed upon their father the label of Absentminded Professor. He frequently, albeit inadvertently, committed such social gaffes, and they had long since grown used to it. Rather than being embarrassed by his forgetfulness, they had, on some level, jointly "chosen" to label it as a kind of endearing trait. Their story: This busy man, of whom we're so proud (and who was indeed a renowned expert in the field of research biology) was long on inspiration if a little short on common sense. It didn't mean he was uncaring or irresponsible, or that he was a "skinflint" who didn't want to pick up the tab and was searching for an excuse.

Notice that this "story" (accurate or not) is important to the family's sense of well-being. Had they perceived Father's behavior otherwise, it might have led to endless frustration for them. What his future daughter-in-law did not know is that this gentleman's inability to pay for the dinner (which all had agreed in advance was a duty that fell to the groom's side) was not *aimed* at her or her family. It was merely a continuation of the ongoing dynamics that had been in place for decades.

The same goes for the engaged woman who grew so agitated when her in-laws-to-be pushed for a macrobiotic wedding menu. Her new family's "story," as she found out in time, was "We're in tip-top condition and will all live to be a hundred." Likewise, for the woman whose future mother- and father-in-law appeared at her chic country club outfitted in sweatsuits. Their family story was—and remains—"We're a casual, carefree, fun-loving bunch." To be sure, at times their casualness and laid-back attitude still annoys their daughter-in-law. But she no longer takes it personally—and she is usually prepared for their unwillingness to deck themselves out in finery the way her family likes to.

To be engaged is to enter boldly into *terra incognita*. And there's no question that facing the many unknowns your new family embodies is anxiety provoking. But on the plus side, you have a wonderful opportunity now to investigate and scope out the situation. As a newcomer at family gatherings, you're not generally expected to say *too* much. Which is not a bad arrangement, when you think about it. It's far more important that you see and hear and process that information. Once you learn your new family's customs, habits, rules, values, and "stories," you will be able to carve a niche for yourself with greater ease.

DEALING WITH CLINGERS, CRITICS, AND CONTROLLERS

Naturally, acclimating yourself to any new family civilization requires tolerance and flexibility. But let's face it, some situations are more difficult than others. And you're not a saint. (Who is?)

So, what do you do if your future family really pushes you to the limits of your patience? Suppose they are Clingers, who really do take over your place for that Monday-night football game and exercise "squatter's rights"—coming back for Tuesday-night basketball, Wednesday-night wrestling, and so on. Suppose they are Critics, who hold nothing back when it comes to airing their feelings about your short skirts or your mother's girth. Or suppose they are Controllers, who not only want you to do what they want (wedding-wise or otherwise) but who bother and browbeat you—or perhaps even try to bribe you—until you feel you have no choice but to capitulate.

Certainly the first thing you must do is remember that, like your family, chances are that members of the groom's family are experiencing separation anxiety at the thought of his changing his relationship to *them* by taking on a wife. Some of them may try harder than others to enact self-protective measures to prevent themselves from experiencing the full force of the blow. They may behave in a proprietary manner toward your fiancé, or convince themselves that you are not so very wonderful as he thinks (i.e., not so very threatening to them), imagining, on some level, that these tactics will enable them to "hold on" to your fiancé.

Your understanding of their possible motives here won't keep their behavior from being any less frustrating, and it won't keep you from feeling miffed. But at least some glimmer of comprehension and compassion on your part may keep your natural defensiveness from swinging over into a full-scale counterattack.

Once you have restrained yourself from going on the offensive, you can build your defense more constructively. And you can calm down enough to avail yourself of some of the following strategies:

AVOIDING THE REBUTTAL SYNDROME

As with your partner himself, you do have an entitlement to voice a protest if your prospective in-laws behave in ways that really push your buttons. But it's wise to do so without inciting a big fuss.

It's always a good idea to try to be diplomatic and, if at all possible, to preface your request with some kind of praise or at least acknowledgment of their point of view, as in "It's nice having you stop by . . . but I need to get to sleep early." Or "It's nice of you to offer to pay for a macrobiotic caterer, but my family and I don't care for that kind of food."

Now be prepared for their rebuttal, as in:

"Oh, heck you're so young. You don't need much sleep. Live a little" or "You don't know what you're missing. The chef we have in mind knows four hundred ways to cook soybeans."

At this juncture, of course, you feel the need to rebut right back. And on you could go—getting nowhere. But what you're after here is not a persistent debate, just a way of making your point pleasantly yet firmly. So instead, simply *acknowledge* their rejoinder (rather than quarreling with it) and then repeat (or slightly rephrase) what you've already said without taking the bait. As in:

"I know rumor has it that young people are night owls, but

it's early to bed for me" or "It's amazing what can be done with soy, but my family will not enjoy that sort of meal."

Now they are less likely to dissent *ad infinitum,* for you have not given them much opening to do so.

HOLD YOUR TONGUE, DON'T BITE IT

Sometimes a Critic will say something that you can't help but hear as "fightin' words." And your impulse may well be to let loose and retaliate. Mentally you agitate: "My skirts are *not* too short, and what business is it of theirs anyhow? And who do they think they *are* saying anything about my dear old mother? It's the height of rudeness to disparage her. They're not fit to sit at her table."

Well, right you are. But you certainly needn't be a Nobel Peace Prize winner to realize that responding this way isn't going to get you very far in winning over these very—shall we say—*challenging* future in-laws. And even if you don't wish to win them over (the truth is that whether you wish it or not, in some cases you may never entirely succeed), you at least want to neutralize their input enough so that it doesn't jeopardize your impending nuptials and the solidity of your marriage. Clearly the way to do that is not to fight fire with a blaze of your own.

So, yes, you do need to hold your tongue and resist lambasting them. But don't *bite* your tongue—by which I mean don't assault yourself as a consequence of your own silence.

A lot of people under stress (and as the future daughter-in-law of a Critic you clearly qualify) seem to feel they have only two choices when provoked. They either attack others or attack themselves. If they choose the latter course, they may actually internalize the criticism to which they are not verbally responding: "Maybe my skirts *are* too short. I'm probably not respectable enough for them. My mother *is* a bit of a tub. I'm so embarrassed—and I'll probably end up overweight like her too."

It may sound extreme, but it's more common than you may realize to let your self-esteem take a beating when there's no immediate, appropriate outlet for ventilating hurt feelings. To weather the stormy prewedding period during which difficult future in-laws may tax you, remember to be as kind to yourself as possible. And let your self-esteem grow from the knowledge that you are mature enough to act out of enlightened self-interest and strong enough to resist the urge to act impulsively.

KEEP COMMUNICATION LINES OPEN

Finally, no matter how irritated you may get with Clingers, Critics, or Controllers, try not to encourage your husband-to-be to turn against his kin and estrange himself from them. Certainly you want to know that you come first with your mate, and if you feel that is not the case, you should clarify with him what your expectations are regarding this. For you and he are starting a new family of your own, and you have every right to anticipate the pleasure and satisfaction of being each other's primary consideration.

But if your fiancé is tempted to go so far as to sever all ties to his kin, know that this does not bode well for the bond you two are forging. As the well-known family therapist Murray Bowen has noted, grown children who have what he calls an "emotional cutoff" from their family of origin place their own marriages in jeopardy. Their inability or unwillingness to tolerate frustration and work through their issues with their parents is an indication that those very issues are prone to resurface as they create their own family.[1]

On some level—especially if your future in-laws are exceptionally contentious, intrusive, or manipulative—it's understandable that part of you may think, "Who needs the aggravation?" Obviously you don't need it. But you may need your in-laws at some point—and the aggravation may simply be part of the package. No one is saying you two have to spend lots of time with difficult family members, or pander to them, or pretend to be their best pals, or take their advice or their money or anything else. But if you keep the lines of communication open and remain at least civil to one another, you will not burn any bridges. And, who knows, one day, your in-laws may mellow.

YOU'VE GOT TO HAVE FRIENDS

Now we must address another element of your future husband's entourage—his friends. Just about everyone comes with friends attached, and all in all that's a very good thing. You would probably be a little nervous if your fiancé had no one he felt close to, liked to talk to, or enjoyed spending time with. If that were the case, you might wonder about his ability to sustain a positive relationship.

The question is, will his friends become your friends? In some cases the answer is probably yes. To some extent you and they are likely to mesh quite nicely. Indeed you may meet some of his friends and immediately experience an agreeable sense of *déjà vu,* as though they're people already known to you on some level. When that's the case, a sense of comfort and ease pervades the atmosphere.

But certainly there may be friends of your fiancé's that rub you the wrong way. Among them:

• *The Gossip*—whose inability to keep a confidence is so legendary that you've nicknamed him Deep Throat.
• *The Lecher*—who might literally try to rub you the wrong way, until you read him the riot act and threaten to tell his girlfriend(s).
• *The Sports Fiend*—who simply can't imagine why your man would rather spend time with you than with a pay-per-view hookup of a middleweight bout, and frequently says so to your face.
• *The Challenger*—who insists he knows more than anyone

about anything and who is wont to turn a friendly game of
Scrabble into an all-night dictionary hunt for the word *yurgle*,
which he *knows* is legitimate.

• *The Sulking Single*—who is miserable that his good
buddy is engaged to be wed while he himself continues to
strike out on the playing field of love.

• *The Crabby Couple*—whose public displays of disaffec-
tion, including—but not limited to—food fights, are so
flamboyant that you only dine out with them in lobster em-
poriums, where you know you will be outfitted with a protec-
tive bib. (They come complete with a large repertoire of
Reasons Why You Two Should Never Get Married and Are
Making the Biggest Mistake of Your Lives.)

Chances are that as you get to know (and not love) these
friends, your Pre-Marital Syndrome stress will soar as you
contemplate a lifetime of being tethered to them. You may
experience some unsettling thoughts concerning the nature of
your partner's taste in humans. You may also begin to scrutinize your fiancé's character for signs that underneath his pre-
sumed personality there may lurk resemblances to these
lower-down-the-food-chain chums.

The first thing you should know about such questionable
types is that, somehow or other, at least a few of them seem
to end up in most everyone's stable of buddies. Who knows
why? Perhaps because the generosity of the human spirit is
boundless. Perhaps because once you share enough college
hangovers with someone, you can't figure out how to tell them
to "go away." The point is such dubious pals are rarely allotted
to only one member of a couple. If asked, your partner would
probably be able to select a similar list of offenders from
among the ranks of *your* friends.

The second thing you should know is that, believe it or
not, each of his friends who in your eyes merits dubious
distinction probably offers something to your mate that he

would say enhances his life in some way. It could be anything. Perhaps the two of them share a special interest that bonds them (Cubist art, foreign policy, heavy metal). Perhaps there are certain activities they enjoy sharing (shooting baskets, shooting skeet). Perhaps in private these "bothersome" friends turn out to be good listeners and serve as trusted sounding boards when your fiancé has something on his mind.

But perhaps you'll never even be quite sure what the attraction is for your fiancé. Well, so what? The most important thing you need to know is that if he finds value in his friends, you need to respect that no matter how you feel about them.

Certainly this does not mean you have to spend an inordinate amount of time with them or extend yourself far beyond the realm of appropriate courtesy and congeniality. In fact, there's nothing wrong with making it clear to your beau that after having given these friends a try and having found them not your cup of tea, you wouldn't mind if he spent time with them by himself. You might offer to do the same with friends of yours he's not crazy about.

Maybe a part of you is resistant to this approach. After all, you're getting married. Doesn't that mean you're supposed to socialize as a couple all the time?

N-O.

It's completely healthy and desirable to spend some time with your own friends and to encourage him to spend time with his. Healthy because it will help keep you both from demanding way too much of each other. No single individual can possibly be all things to any other individual. But among your own friends you can generally find a potpourri of temperaments with which to mesh diverse aspects of yourself (a friend you can be rowdy with when you're in the mood to kick up your heels; a pal you can be contemplative with when you're in the mood to meditate).

On the other hand, if you don't endure your fiancé's

spending time with his friends during your engagement, and if you don't spend time with yours, you are setting yourselves up for a fall. With all the intense, complicated emotions you are experiencing right now, it's a wonderful idea to take periodic breaks from one another—even if they are simply in the form of a night off with your buddies.

Friends should be cherished commodities. You are both lucky to have them. The only caveat you should both be aware of is that when you are really angry at each other—so angry that you're thinking of calling the wedding off—friends may tend to stoke the fires, either out of unconscious agendas of their own or simply out of a long-standing habit of reinforcing a pal's point of view. Just take their commiseration with a grain of salt, and remember that you don't always have to take their advice, even if you solicit it.

COMMINGLING

There's still one more aspect of your entourage dilemma to cover. Even once you and your fiancé come to terms with each other's friends and families, you will still have to grapple with whether or not they'll come to terms with each other.

Many an apprehensive bride-to-be has tormented herself with the very idea that someday, probably before the wedding (and, if not, then certainly *at* it) her entourage and his entourage will have to commingle.

In the old days this would have likely happened long before a betrothal took place. For the most part, people tended to marry within their social and economic class to people who lived in close proximity. And not that many young adults would dream of marrying someone whose family and group of friends did not "fit" with theirs.

Today, for many lovers on the verge of wedlock, no such unwritten rules apply, and fewer such considerations merit serious attention. An engaged couple in Baltimore may have families scattered to the four winds, with a wedding bringing relatives in from L.A., Cleveland, Boston, Miami, Baja, and the Yukon. Even some of their friends may be far-flung, what with some ex-high school chums and erstwhile roommates still living in their hometowns and college towns and others moving on elsewhere.

In certain cases those friends and relations may get along swimmingly, regardless of whether or not they have much in common on a surface level. In other cases they may blend as smoothly as motor oil and Evian water.

Your separate contingencies may consist, respectively, of ultraright Republicans and diehard Democrats, deer hunters and animal-rights organizers, charity-ball hostesses and charity cases. They may see eye to eye on very few things. Or in some cases they may agree on only one thing: that you and your beloved are an obvious mismatch.

So be it.

Granted, it would all be very nice indeed if your brood and his brood would share the instantaneous rapport that you two kindled at the start. Or at least be nice to each other. In most cases you can usually count on mutual civility as opposed to Hatfield-McCoy shoot-outs or Montague-Capulet psychodramas. But don't get your hopes way up. And don't imagine it's your task to make everyone relish everyone else's company. That's simply an impossible project to undertake.

At times it may be difficult to resist the temptation to bridge the gap between even your most reluctant and recalcitrant friends and family members—so difficult that you won't resist it at all. Undoubtedly you will at some point plunge headlong into arranging intimate dinner parties across family lines, or fixing people up on dates from "your side" and "his side."

Okay, so you tried. Now your Aunt Rhoda, the society matron, and his Uncle Elmo, the demolition-derby driver, are struggling to find something to say after "Pass the salt," while his brother, George, the Quaker, is being shouted down by your brother, Buster, an officer of the National Rifle Association. Now his college roommate and your best friend from the office are glumly facing the prospect of an evening together after having classified their initial reaction to each other as "hate at first sight." Everyone will survive of course, but *really* you didn't have to try so hard.

Contrary to what you may think, the success of your marriage cannot necessarily be predicted by how well your respective loved ones get along. As is often the case, such an assumption tends to be based on a fear that has no basis in reality.

FEAR: "I fixed my best friend up with his best friend, and it was a disaster. And after meeting each other once, our mutually unimpressed parents even had to be prodded into exchanging Christmas cards! That must be a bad omen for the two of us."

FALLACY: You think your best friends should get along because your girlfriend is so much like you and your fiancé's buddy is so much like him. You think your parents should get along because each set of them produced one of you, and *you* hit it off big-time.

REALITY: Regarding your friends, look again. Your best friend is not likely to be your carbon copy, nor your future husband's pal his clone. Friends tend to complement one another's style, not mimic it. And even if there are similarities between the two women and two men involved here, there's no accounting for timing, chemistry, and all the myriad ingredients that go into the stew of attraction.

As for your parents, come on, now! Ever since the dawn of adolescence you've probably prided yourself on being different from them in any number of ways.

That probably goes ditto for your fiancé. Now you're upset because you think all the parents involved here should react exactly the way their children do. Why the change of heart?

REMEDY: Whether your friends despise each other on sight or fly off to Vegas leaving you two stuck with the dinner check on a double date is basically irrelevant. Whether your parents decide to join up for a golf foursome or give each other the cold shoulder is not wildly relevant either. It is not your job to pair people off as if you were the cruise director on Noah's ark. If such matches work out, fine. If not, it's likely you'll have amusing anecdotes to tell your children and their children.

But wait a minute. Who said anything about children? Well, you may not have said it yet. But chances are you're thinking along these lines. Which is the subject of our next chapter.

CHAPTER SEVEN

FAMILY MATTERS, FUTURE TENSE ("*HE'S* GOING TO FATHER *MY* CHILDREN?")

First comes love, then comes marriage;
Then comes ——— with a baby carriage.
—*SCHOOLYARD RHYME*

When you were a girl conjuring up a mental picture of the time when you would grow up and be wed, it's very likely that a child or two was included in your futuristic scenario. Now wedding time is fast approaching. And though it may be years before you decide to have children, if indeed you ever do, you'll probably begin contemplating the *prospect* of your own parenthood not long after an engagement ring is placed upon your finger.

Sometimes this kind of anticipation takes only a vague shape, but it's not unusual for a certain amount of concrete discussion and negotiation to be done even at this early stage of the game. And, along with everything else that's going on, it can cause quite a stir of emotions.

I recall counseling an engaged couple, Ellen and Jack, one evening when their discussion veered to the prospect of children in their future life together. Both agreed they would like to have children, and both said two would be an ideal number. (So far, so good, for as we'll see, such nitty-gritty issues are often major sticking points.) Soon, however, Ellen asked, in a somewhat playful manner, whether Jack would be prepared to load and unload the diaper pail. Her boyfriend laughed and said, "Thank goodness for disposable diapers."

Upon which a look of horror and revulsion crossed the face of the bride-to-be. To her mind, her future husband had been unveiled as an environmental menace. What kind of values was he going to teach *her* kids, anyhow? Was he going to let them litter? Would he buy them politically incorrect toys packaged in those awful Styrofoam peanuts? Would he forget to teach them about recycling? And, what's more, was he going to be one of those dads who—like his own father—came home from work and put his feet up while *she* followed her job with a "second shift" as housekeeper and homework helper? Oh, she could see it all now!

Needless to say, Ellen's fiancé was less than thrilled to be characterized as a planetary polluter and, as he put it, "an insensitive chauvinist oinker," let alone to be accused of potentially passing these dubious codes of ethics on to unsuspecting offspring.

And what did she mean by calling them *her* children, anyhow!? Obviously Ellen was going to be one of those domineering mothers, like *her* mother, Jack hypothesized, whose sole goal in life was to keep her brood tied to her apron strings and to make them think the way she thought about everything—including her silly, unrealistic do-gooder causes.

Ultimately this prenuptial brouhaha calmed down long enough for the twosome to agree that neither of them could "see it all now," but that, clearly, each of them had some fears about future family life that had best be addressed—albeit in a more reasonable manner.

The fact is anyone who did not grow up in a picture-perfect family has some natural anxiety about what kind of parent they'll be and also about how their mate will handle this awesome responsibility. But imagining the future is often hampered by hanging on to the past.

If your experience of family life—or your experience of your fiancé's family—is less than idyllic, does that mean you are both doomed to repeat history? And if your mate has a few flaws (and, need I remind you, everyone's does) does that mean he isn't fit to father?

These are issues worth exploring, but before we do, let's go back to some nitty-gritty issues that may be causing you and your fiancé prenuptial friction.

BIRDS DO IT, BEES DO IT

Jack and Ellen did not reach a bump in the road in their negotiations concerning children until their discussion turned to how their kids would be raised. You may hit them even sooner, as you and your fiancé broach such questions as: Will you have kids at all? And how many kids will you have?

Often such topics are approached circuitously. Picture this: You and your beau are strolling down the street on the way to, say, pick out your silverware pattern and invitation typeface. Diapers, formula, and family planning are the farthest things from your conscious mind. Then you pass by a particularly enchanting infant being perambulated by its proud parents. And, *boom,* just like that, your expectation meter starts to run.

Perhaps you are a Righteous Romantic whose visceral response is, "I want two stunning children, a darling little boy and, two years later, a precious little girl. Then we really will be the perfect family."

Perhaps you are a Teary Tester, who feels trapped by the prospect of wailing tots linking you irreversibly to this exasperating future husband of yours. (And who happens to recall a pearl of Mark Twain cynicism: "Familiarity breeds contempt—and children.")

Perhaps you are a Halfway Hysteric, whose frequent dreams of future familial bliss are occasionally interrupted by nightmares of custody battles to come should your marriage bite the dust.

Or perhaps you are none of the above Pre-Marital Syndrome types, but have a strong gut reaction (as babies are wont to induce) regardless.

Now glance over at your fiancé. How has he reacted to this tiny bundle of infantile cuteness being paraded before him? Do you think he's thinking, "Say, that gives *me* an idea"? Or, "Yikes, I hope we're stocked up on birth control devices." Or: "I wonder how much that stroller costs. Thank goodness we don't have to worry about *that* for a long time." Or do you suspect that he is oblivious to the adorable scenery and has focused instead on some other matter of critical importance, such as what he wants for lunch?

Maybe you don't have any idea *what* he's thinking. In any case, you shouldn't assume you know unless you're told—for you may be mistaken. What we clearly have here is another significant area in which to share expectations.

While no one expects you to have your whole life blueprinted at the present moment (that's correct, Righteous Romantics, not even *you,* paragons of organization and efficiency, can predict and control everything), if you look into your heart, which is often where Back-Burnered or Out-of-Sight expectations seem to generate, you probably have some notion of what size and shape you would like your future family to take. And so does your partner.

But what if those notions don't jive with one another? What if you picture two kids and he pictures one, or five, or a baker's dozen? What if you hear only the ticking of your biological clock, whereas he hears only the rattle of chains he associates with parenthood's attendant loss of freedom? What if you want to postpone starting a family while you ascend the corporate ladder or finish your master's degree, while he simply can't wait to start buying Gund bears and to see you decked out in maternity frocks that *you* dread will make you look like a beached whale?

Problem? Well, more so if you don't talk about it all than if you do. It's amazing how many couples I've seen enter into marriage *assuming* their spouse agreed with them about what the configuration of their family ought to be, as well as about the timing of starting a family. In due course they discover, much to their mutual dismay, that their assumptions were unfounded. The engagement period is, without doubt, the appropriate time to put those cards on the table.

In many cases couples who discuss future families during the course of engagement will find that, for each of them, the actual idea of starting a family is somewhat vague—a pleasant "someday" sort of thing. They think they want to have children, but aren't sure exactly how many children they want to have or *when* they want to have them. Such tentativeness is perfectly natural.

Erik Erikson, the renowned developmental psychologist, described child rearing as an important stage of adult development. Mature man, he said, needs to experience being needed and also requires "guidance and encouragement" from his own offspring.[1] But life's stages unfold in their own good time, and perhaps at this time a pleasant but amorphous desire to have children at some point is all your already overtaxed premarital psyches can assimilate.

Yet even if the precise *what*s and *when*s of parenthood are still unformed, some related concerns may nevertheless creep into your mind. You may be starting to wonder *how* you'll do as parents.

OLD PATTERNS, NEW OPTIONS

In a now-famous 1975 Ann Landers reader's poll, 70 percent of fifty thousand responding parents said that if they'd had it to do over, they would not have had kids. But in a study by well-known pollster Daniel Yankelovich, 90 percent said they *would* take the parental plunge again.[2] Though the conflicting messages of these surveys may seem difficult to reconcile, they appear to reflect two sides of the same coin. In fact one could probably elicit such dissimilar results by asking the very same sets of parents this very same question on different days.

Having children offers up the potential for a tremendous amount of joy, as well as a tremendous amount of frustration. (It will make wedding planning look like a day at the beach.) Even imagining being responsible for brand-new lives may give you an overwhelming sense of insecurity as you ask yourself incredulously, "Who, me?"

The bride-to-be, of course, may have yet another source of insecurity. Gazing upon her fundamentally imperfect mate, scion of a fundamentally flawed family, she may wonder, "Who, *him*?"

Suppose, she muses, he turns out like *his* parents? You know, those officious, controlling parents? Or the critical parents, who will barely let you breathe without suggesting a better way to inhale? Or the intrusive parents, who seem to have forgotten that children should be encouraged to have a life of their own? Or the self-righteous, or hot-tempered, or demanding, or guilt-invoking or in some other way objectionable parents she has come to tolerate but hardly to adore?

Even if she genuinely likes her future in-laws (and many women really do), wouldn't it be just like her husband-to-be to carry on the one or two annoying family traits to which she'd simply rather not expose a child? (For example, will he be, like his own father, a dad who checks out of family life for the greater part of football season, or who *never* misses an opportunity to extol the virtues of hanging on to a dollar?) Well, possibly.

And possibly this future husband has similar fears about his bride-to-be. He wonders, Will she be like her own mother who is, in his opinion, a nervous and overprotective parent, a proprietary parent who doesn't seem to want to let her kids grow up (let alone get married)?

In the scenario that began this chapter we saw a couple, Ellen and Jack, in mid-premarital quarrel, tell each other they knew, they just *knew,* what sort of parent each other would make. A bad one, that's what sort! An oblivious father, who scarfs pretzels and watches *Wheel of Fortune* while his toddler sets the living room on fire. A drill sergeant of a mother, who won't let the kids out of her sight.

These images did not just spring forth out of nowhere. In both cases each partner was voicing a fear that was based on his or her impression of the other's parents (albeit blown up to extreme dimensions). They felt certain that similarities in parenting style would be inescapable. For they could not envision creating family dynamics that were unlike the ones already in existence.

Did their fears have any basis in reality? Some.

It does seem uncanny how very often children grow to mirror the parenting behavior of their own mothers and fathers—even if that behavior was frustrating to them, or something they swore they'd never repeat. If you've ever heard your mother's words coming out of your mouth, spoken in a tone you never thought you'd hear escape your own lips ("Get those feet off my couch!"), you know what this means.

Few of us are immune to the current of maternal power that trips such switches, at least now and again. We simply spend so many formative years under the influence of our parents, we are bound unwittingly to internalize certain of their aspects.

So, if you have the idea that your beau may have a tendency to father the way his own father did, that idea is not wholly misbegotten—any more than is *his* idea that, in certain ways, you may be prone to re-create your mother's style of mothering. But now the good news: Keep in mind that we internalize many of our parents' positive traits as well as their exasperating ones. It's simply the latter we tend to notice more because of their frustrating nature.

It's highly unlikely that every aspect of your future husband's family life will be a negative influence, any more than every influence from your family would prove negative. (His father may have been relatively uninvolved in daily parenting chores, but always available for emotional support; your mother may have been a bit overbearing, but also the role model for your energy and drive.)

As for the aspects of parental styles that could potentially pack a negative wallop, it is nowhere written in stone that such batons must be handed from one generation to the next. The forces of history *are* mutable when there is an awareness of their existence and a conscious resolve to mitigate them by thinking before acting. Give your future spouse some credit that he will avail himself of these tools, just as you may avail yourself of them. Who knows? Together you may reinvent the wheel.

A QUESTION OF VALUES

Going back to the story of Ellen and Jack one final time, there's another element to their quarrel that requires exploring. Some of their fears regarding each other's "suitability" for parenthood did not have to do with potential hand-me-down behaviors but with concerns about each other's values.

Values, whether we consciously think about them or not, are the basis of many of our attitudes, preferences, and decisions. Values are things we believe in, would stand up for, and very well might fight for. Yet while some people are extremely vocal and quite clear about their values (Patrick Henry made no bones about it when he said, "Give me liberty or give me death"), others are more circumspect. Perhaps they have rarely given any formal thought to what their values are and so are unable to articulate them clearly. Perhaps they don't want to risk any sort of controversy.

When two people are courting, they may have yet other reasons for choosing not to verbalize certain of their values. Sometimes they really can't imagine that their beloved will disagree with them. Consequently they take for granted an accord that simply isn't there. Sometimes they *wish* the accord was there and don't want to deal with the fact that, deep down, they know it's actually not.

In Jack and Ellen's case, the bride-to-be was incensed by her husband's remark about disposable diapers. Offhand as it was, to her it belied a fundamental disregard for issues about which she felt passionately. It bespoke what she considered an "irresponsible" attitude on her fiancé's part that she'd recognized on some level, but had tried assiduously to ignore. As for the future groom, this occasioned an opportunity to voice some irritation he'd been harboring (but not verbalizing) about what he considered Ellen's overly zealous dedication to various environmental causes. He called her, in none too glowing intonations, a "silly do-gooder" and, in so doing, devalued her.

Ellen's devotion to the cause of a cleaner planet and the fact that Jack was not as conscientious as she when it came to cultivating earth-saving habits was a difference that could conceivably have gone unaddressed for quite some time, what with personal rather than global issues clamoring for this couple's attention in the hectic premarital months. But the prospect of parenting the next generation crystallized the matter. Just how "green" was Jack and Ellen's household going to be, anyhow?

What this couple came to realize was that it was neither

possible nor necessary (nor even desirable) to make such policy decisions beforehand. At this point most things were open to negotiation and renegotiation. Compromise or possibly even conversion (a relatively rare marital occurrence wherein one party "sees the light") might be the ultimate result. But maybe not. Maybe this couple, despite their underlying affection for each other, would always engage in a tug-of-war over "green" issues.

In your relationship, too, certain differences in value systems may exist. It's more common than you might imagine for liberals and conservatives, or doves and militarists, to merge in the name of love. And none should doubt that the annals of contemporary marriage are replete with scrupulously honest taxpayers joined to diehard loophole seekers, yellow-light runners to strict speed-limit observers, public-television watchers to made-for-TV-movie junkies, heaven seekers to reincarnation believers, neatness freaks to clothes-on-the-floor enthusiasts, and nightly flossers to halfhearted brushers. Due to passion's capacity to overwhelm them, smitten lovers may simply choose not to notice such differences in one another's preferences, principles and approach to the world.

But if you are among this large segment of the engaged population, do not despair—even if you are reasonably certain that parenthood for the two of you looms not too far down the road. Contrary to what you may think, offering your children differing points of view and alternate outlooks on life is not the worst thing in the world. In fact it has its pluses. Once again, your fear could be based on a faulty assumption.

FEAR: "If my partner and I are not of 'one mind,' we will probably end up raising woefully confused kids with no decent value system at all. Why, getting married could prove a disservice not only to us but to the entire human race."

FALLACY: You believe your kids will be poor lost

souls unless you and your mate are in basic agreement on virtually everything. You're not giving these hypothetical offspring of yours much latitude, are you?

REALITY: Often kids can benefit from being exposed to differing ideas and temperaments. They can thus learn to adjust to a world where such divergence is in fact the norm. They can also learn to make discriminating choices and develop values that are comfortable for *them,* perhaps incorporating elements of both parents' belief systems. If that's not enough to convince you, family therapist Murray Bowen has pointed out that too much parental "we-ness" can be detrimental to children, who may experience an unwavering unified parental front as a hopeless "two-against-one" situation.[3]

REMEDY: Certainly it's tough to come to the realization that you and the person you are about to marry may not stand for the same things. Granted, it is a sign that you and he will not always be in complete harmony with one another and that your children may not grow up to embrace uncategorically every pearl of wisdom you have to offer. But if you want total harmony, you ought to forgo the idea of creating a marriage and parenthood altogether and join a glee club instead.

It's a naive idea that families should always resonate with synergy, and one that will only lead you to endless disappointment should you cling to it.

Marriage is going to change you in certain significant ways that you can't foresee. And having children with your spouse will change your relationship—though just how it will is somewhat unpredictable. You and your partner may find you come to share some points of view you never dreamed you would, but there are likely to be surprises in the other direction as well—that is, you may begin in accord on something, only to find one of you has a change of heart. Met with hard-headed resistance, such developments can knock you and your union off-balance. Met with tolerance, they may, on occasion, drive you round the bend—but at the same time they can add spice and zest to the twists and turns of your wedded journey.

POSTSCRIPT: THE NAME GAME

This chapter requires a postscript, since there is a somewhat related topic that often arises when engaged couples are contemplating the prospect of having children—if it has not surfaced already. That is the issue of whether or not the bride-to-be will take her husband's surname.

These days, as you are doubtless aware, it is socially acceptable for, say, a Miss Priscilla Smurth to remain a Smurth, even after marrying, say, a Reginald Fleeflicker. It is also completely legal, for no state in the union requires a woman to take her husband's name once she weds.[4]

Of course if she so chooses, she may become Mrs. Fleeflicker. And she may even choose to become Mrs. (or Ms.) Smurth-Fleeflicker. It's common to be slightly befuddled by the pros and cons of these various options, and therefore many engaged women simply delay a decision for a time.

But once she begins to envision a bouncy little boy or girl Fleeflicker or Smurth-Fleeflicker down the road, our hypothetical Miss Smurth may decide to give the whole matter more weight. Indeed she may, like many of her fellow engaged women, begin to mildly obsess on the quandary it creates.

What should she do? What are the consequences of keeping or surrendering or modifying the name with which she was born?

On the practical side, to become a Fleeflicker is to necessitate the countless clerical chores involved in altering one's passport, driver's license, car registration, checks and credit cards, business cards and stationery—and in notifying one's insurance carriers, mail carriers, travel agent, payroll department, alumni organizations and professional organizations. On the emotional side, it may instigate the uneasy feeling that she's somehow disappeared.

The first time an old friend's letter arrives three months late (it's been making the rounds trying to track her down) and invites her to a reunion now long past, the new Mrs. Flee-flicker, née Smurth, may experience a twinge of resentment. And the first time she loses out on a deal at work because, perhaps, an erstwhile client could not locate her, she may hit the ceiling. What kind of a silly tradition is this anyway? You don't catch men ditching the name *they've* carried around for several decades. Who needs the aggravation, who needs to invite an identity crisis in the midst of all these other adjustments?

On the other hand, for some women this level of inconvenience and existential angst tends to wane sometime during the first year or so of marriage. Our newlywed may grow accustomed to being a Fleeflicker, which, as she settles into the rhythm of marriage, seems more and more to "fit." On the plus side, she may have the feeling (as may her spouse) that they are somehow more "unified" and that their status is clearer than if she'd taken the path of least resistance and remained a Smurth. Many women who do choose to change their surname do so because it is important to them (and often to their partner as well) to make as public a statement as possible about the nature of their bond.

To become a Smurth-Fleeflicker may, to some, seem like the best of all possible solutions. King Solomon could not have come up with a more judicious compromise, right? Except the clerical chores do not diminish and in some senses become more complex. Chances are, for example that many credit cards do not have enough room for this sizable surname (most limit the number of characters used in one's name to twenty or so) and do not allow the use of hyphens. Indeed one may notice, after a time, that many people and institutions seem to have a firm resistance to composite names. To use one is absolutely your prerogative, but it may require forbearance in the extreme.

Looking ahead to when the kiddies come adds new elements to this awesome decision. Should Miss Smurth remain a Smurth after giving birth to little Fleeflickers, that will likely incite a certain amount of confusion among day-care administrators, teachers, and PTA officials down the line, as everyone wonders just which little tyke belongs to whom. And though by keeping her maiden name, this woman avoided undergoing the identity crisis she dreaded, she may now fear fostering such a crisis in her kids.

Should Miss Smurth become Mrs. Smurth-Fleeflicker, and bestow hyphens on her children as well, she may avoid such confusion. But I've seen many brides about to choose this course of action get cold feet when they begin to wonder what happens if their little Smurth-Fleeflicker grows up to wed someone *else* whose name is hyphenated and their four-surname children grow up to do the same. The thought of a potential crop of grandchildren named Smurth-Fleeflicker-Smith-Brown-Vladistock-Bartolucci-Klein-O'Malley puts a damper on their modern nineties approach to the name game.

But this is not to imply that the only "right" choice to make when considering kids is to take your future husband's name. There is no "right" choice. Only one that feels most comfortable to you or that seems to you the least complicated—on a practical and emotional level—of several complicated options.

If you surrender your maiden name, be prepared to mourn it for a period of time. Even if it's a cumbersome moniker you've often wished you could shed, it's how you've been addressed by others and known yourself for as long as you've been on this earth. And be prepared for the inevitable, and sometime maddening, paperwork maze.

If you keep your own surname, be prepared to suffer the slings and arrows of tax accountants, mortgage brokers, and airline and hotel clerks, who can't seem to get it through their heads why you and your spouse would be so obstinate and contrary as to make their lives more difficult. Be prepared as well to to tolerate possible barbs from parties who ought to know better than to question your judgment in this very personal matter, but who may see fit to anyhow (possibly your mother or your mother-in-law, maybe even your more "traditional" friends, who swear they'd *never* do as you've done).

If on some level it seems unfair that you have to make this choice, it *is* unfair. Men don't have to, and if they did, the system might be more accommodating (cross-referenced phone books perhaps?). But, beginning in the late nineteenth century, feminists worked hard to challenge the confounding and conflicting case law in this area so that you could have options. Avail yourself of them as you see fit. And don't feel you have to apologize to anyone.

CHAPTER EIGHT

LAST-CHANCE
FANTASIES

*If a man will begin with certainties, he will
end in doubts; but if he be content to begin
with doubts, he will end up with certainties.*
—*FRANCIS BACON*,
ADVANCEMENT OF LEARNING

Now you're at a point where you've thought about the upside
and the downside of marriage. You've fought, and reconciled,
over wedding matters and money matters and family matters,
and who knows what else. You've endured exasperation and
frustration, but have tried your best to exude grace under
pressure.

Often that grace has triumphed. *Somehow* you've gotten
your future in-laws to accept the idea that you won't be calling
them Mommy and Daddy. Somehow you've gotten your own
parents to stop calling your fiancé "What's-his-name." Somehow, after spending hours trying your married name on for
size by doodling it over and over on a legal pad, you've
resolved your dilemma, one way or the other, about what to
call yourself.

On top of all this, somehow you've *finally* decided about
the hors d'oeuvres (shrimp puffs), the bridesmaid dresses (tea-

length, ecru-colored, natural fiber), and the reception music (okay, okay, you'll let Cousin Wayne sing "Feelings" after all).

So now you're set for the big event. More or less.

Except you haven't yet had the requisite bout of Last-Minute-itis. But don't worry, you will.

Last-Minute-itis may sound like the Latin term for some kind of bacterial infection. In fact it is a kind of emotional fever that afflicts approximately 99.999 percent of brides-to-be as they tear off the final calendar page that demarcates the months *before* the wedding from the actual month *of* the wedding.

Its symptoms can include shortness of breath, lightness of head, teeth grinding, heart palpitations, pains in the neck (both literal and figurative), memory loss (*where* is that marriage license? *who* is the best man?), clammy hands, and the proverbial "cold feet." Almost invariably this condition also engenders increased daydreaming. And that daydreaming, interestingly enough, sometimes involves members of the opposite sex who are not—repeat, not—your fiancé.

As your wedding draws closer, such daydreams may arise sheerly out of your mind's meanderings. Perhaps you find yourself ducking out of work early to catch a movie for the eighth time because it features your favorite male lead. Caught up in your (very natural) last-minute doubts about the wisdom of your life-partner choice, you can't help but wonder what it would have been like to wind up with, say, Michael Douglas, William Hurt, or Mel Gibson.

Or perhaps after your "traditional" shower (Tupperware, blenders, monogrammed towels, hats made of bows), some of your more boisterous girlfriends treat you to a risqué night at Chippendale's, where you imagine vividly what it would be like to dally with the especially outstanding specimen of malehood who happens to be bumping and grinding before you as you slurp your third wine spritzer of the evening.

All of this is harmless of course. For too long some

good-natured prenuptial drooling has been the exclusive rite of passage for male bachelors. Now women are going public about their desire—and entitlement—to indulge in the same.

A flight of fancy of erotic nature never hurt any bride-to-be and is in fact a pleasant diversion from worrying about final nuptial details. But there are times during which the romantic-fantasy aspect of Last Minute-itis can be a little more complicated. Because in addition to—or in lieu of—being besotted by movie stars and male dancers, you may find yourself captivated by any one of the plethora of real-life men who suddenly and mysteriously seem to be swarming around you and who come across as especially determined to sweep you off your feet.

Now, your head tells you life is not a romance novel, and certainly your table-mannerless, non-flower-sending, complacent fiancé has not been acting as though it is. But as you edge closer to being a Mrs., suddenly you may feel like a heroine out of the latest Barbara Cartland tome. Because it's a funny thing about getting engaged to one special man: suddenly, you may find yourself extremely desirable to *other* men.

This remarkable phenomenon has prompted many delighted and tantalized (but somewhat guilty and perplexed) brides-to-be to ask themselves the question . . .

WHERE WERE ALL THESE GUYS BEFORE?

It usually starts innocently enough. You stroll up to the office water cooler for a brief break and run into a colleague with whom you have a casual smile-and-nod acquaintance. Today he makes conversation and intense eye contact—for oh, say, an hour and a half.

Or you run into a neighbor in the freezer aisle of the supermarket and find that a friendly chat about the merits of various nonfat dietary desserts evolves into a lengthy heart-to-heart during which he *swears* he can see straight into your soul through those beautiful blue eyes of yours. "So you're getting married," he queries with a dubious note. "Are you *sure* this is what you want?"

Oh, no! Now you're in a pickle. This guy is cute. Real cute. And he's nice, and smart, and so much more *polite* and *sensitive* than . . . than . . . What's-his-name. And he seems *so* interested in you. How come you never really noticed him?

Maybe you're tempted and titillated by the prospect of pursuing a more meaningful relationship with this fascinating character. Hey, maybe it's a sign from above. *Maybe you said yes to the wrong guy.* After all, you've seen *The Philadelphia Story.* Perhaps some similar destiny is meant for you.

But hold on here, your conscience counsels. How can you even ponder such a thing!? Think of the chaos it would cause.

The Righteous Romantic decries cruel fate. She fears that perhaps she's found a "more perfect" love. *But why now?* The invitations are sent, the nonrefundable deposits have been placed, and the gifts have begun to arrive so frequently that she's on a first-name basis with the UPS man. Is it simply too late to undo what's been done? After all, *what will people say?*

The Teary Tester, compelled as she is by this charming and earnest suitor, is reduced to a blubbering heap at the thought of the inevitable farewell speech to her erstwhile fiancé. ("If only you had *really* loved me . . .") Are there enough tissues on the planet to pull this off?

The Halfway Hysteric feels paralyzed by her quandary. She is torn between jumping on the horse of this White Knight of the Water Cooler and riding off into the sunset, or nobly spurning his love and biting her tongue when the minister asks, "Is there anyone here who knows a reason why these two should not wed?"

So, what's a girl to do? If you find yourself in a similar fix, with a would-be suitor in hot pursuit during the very time you're already experiencing the emotional *Sturm und Drang* of Last-Minute-itis, you may find yourself far more bewitched than you might care to admit. There's not a thing wrong with letting your fantasies go where they may. But before you take any irreversible steps, there are a few things you ought to consider, for example . . .

IS HE SINCERE?

At this point you can't rule out the possibility that your amorous co-worker or next-door neighbor has suddenly noticed your many fine attributes and is responding to them at this time (the imminence of your wedding being a mere coincidence). But, not to cast aspersions on your many attractive qualities, one ought not leap to this conclusion. Many members of the opposite sex find a woman who's "taken" irresistible—pretty much because she is not on the open market, so to speak.

Hence you'd be smart to approach all such situations with a healthy dose of caution. Before you leap into anything you may regret, ask yourself if your potential paramour could be one of the following types:

> *The Grandstander:* He's a maker of grand gestures and ostentatious displays. He'll set out to dazzle and delight you in a way that can't help but be noticed by *everyone*—sending you bouquets that dwarf the ones your fiancé *used* to send you, faxing you an invitation to a romantic weekend . . . in the south of France. Perhaps he'll even serenade you from outside your bedroom window. His charming antics can be hard to ignore and even harder to resist. But what this guy really wants is attention—and not just yours but the whole world's.

> *The One-Upper:* He knows your betrothed and—for whatever reasons—loathes your betrothed. He'd do

just about anything to show up your beau and "prove" that he's the better man, including waging a no-holds-barred campaign for your affections. He'll do all he can not only to promote himself but to inflate your case of Last-Minute-itis by subtly disparaging your choice of husband.

The Commitmentphobe: A perennial Don Juan, this guy flits from romance to romance like a hyperactive bee when spring is in bloom. His courtship is mercurial. Just when you think he's settling down to savor one blossom, he's buzzing off in search of a "sweeter" one. Look carefully and you'll see he doesn't love women at all, he just loves the idea of being in love.

If you're not sure whether your suitor fits into one (or more) of these categories, test the waters about his sincerity. Hint that you're taking his advances seriously. But rather than imply you are calling off your wedding for an uncertain future, make him understand that *you simply want to switch grooms.*

If he's a Grandstander, a One-Upper, or a Commitment-phobe, he'll probably break out into a cold sweat and start babbling quasi-incoherently about "not rushing into anything." Remember, what these types want from you has nothing to do with long-term pledges and promises. They want their egos stroked.

LAST-MINUTE LIMERENCE

Of course there is always the possibility that someone who wages a last-minute courtship as your wedding approaches is indeed acting in a heartfelt manner. And you could have the feeling that you are genuinely interested in pursuing a relationship with him. In fact you *can't seem to stop thinking about the possibility*. Now you need to determine what *your* motivations really are.

At this point you ought to know about an emotional phenomenon that psychologist Dorothy Tennov has called limerence.[1] It's a kind of "altered state" that you may be in even now.

Limerence is a storybooklike infatuation with an admired person (Tennov designates this person the limerent object.). It typically involves continuous, intrusive preoccupation (in one's mind there are lots of luscious imaginary dialogues and caresses). There's a palpable longing for actual contact and also—not a big surprise—a tendency to overemphasize the limerent object's positive characteristics.

Limerence feels wonderful. When in its enchanted midst, one has the sense that time is suspended, that nothing matters except the proximity and reciprocity of the admired one. When the limerent object is nearby and attentive, problems, troubles, and inconveniences pale. In their place are bells, whistles, and fireworks.

In many ways, limerence may sound and seem familiar. You've probably experienced it before in your life (most of us do at one time or another). And this state may even remind you of how you felt when you first met the man who is now your fiancé. In some ways it probably is, but there is one distinct difference.

Earlier you read about the three components of love: passion, intimacy, and commitment. Limerence is solely bound up in the passion component, but unlike fully formed love itself, it *never* moves beyond. It never expands to accommodate the stresses and strains of daily life, and it never survives the unmasking process that your current relationship has already begun to weather.

Indeed, part of you probably already surmises that any infatuation you have with another man during Last-Minute-itis is suspect. So why are you feeling this way? Is there something wrong with you?

Not a thing. But as a very-soon-to-be-married woman, you are a ripe candidate for limerence toward a new man (at this seemingly inopportune moment) for several reasons:

It's distracting. There's nothing like daydreams of a storybook romance to take the edge off nagging concerns about your nuptial hairdo, your impending seating-chart disasters (Aunt Betty has just had a major falling-out with Grandma Maude) and the plethora of duplicate wedding gifts you're going to have to return.

It's enthralling. Your limerent object is, for you, a real taboo—a kind of forbidden fruit. Your actually taking up with him would defy social custom. It would be risky, ergo exciting. And after months of dealing with details, details, details, the prospect of such reckless abandon can have understandable appeal.

It's reassuring. The looming prospect of saying the actual words "till death do us part" may make you feel a little old before your time. (What do they mean, *death*?) You want to feel alive, attractive, desirable, *immortal.* Limerence, with its lusty charge, can inject you with a dose of youthful euphoria.

Last but not least, last-minute limerence offers an instinctive mental counterpoint to those lingering doubts about your fiancé's potential as a husband. To the degree that your initial bout of passion with your betrothed has begun to cool and to the degree that you imagine your relationship with your fiancé to be problematical, you will imagine your prospective relationship with your limerent object to be problem-free. (Ha!)

Now, there's nothing wrong with *imagining* this at all. Just keep in mind that you are in the realm of fantasy. The one thing limerence is *not* is durable. In fact, as studies have shown, people in the "postlimerent" state seem unable to clearly remember the very experience that seemed, at the time, so overpowering.[2] Trying to relive a limerent interlude in memory is similar to groping back for specifics of a rapidly dimming dream in the bright light of morning.

As a couple on the verge of marriage, you and your partner have already made a statement to each other and to your friends and family that your relationship has depth and integrity—that it is made of far more stable stuff than idle dreams. You two see each other as a great deal more than sources of immediate gratification and distractions from trying circumstances. What's more, that ring on your finger, those invitations in the mail, have proclaimed that there is lots more than lust in your hearts.

That's not to say that you don't—or won't—at times hanker for each other with cravings approaching those of the time when you first fell in love. In an enduring marriage where both spouses admire, respect, and care for one another—and generally enjoy one another's company—both partners may, now and again, experience surges of heated desire and bask in a kind of romantic "buzz" that feels like limerence.

All well and good. But as a couple you will have to grapple with the married state one day at a time. And there will be many days when your buzz is drowned out by the clamor of other emotions and pressing concerns *du jour*.

That's the difference between life and limerence.

Certainly one can't rule out the incremental outside chance that you are one of those rare women who happened to have discovered your true soul mate days or weeks before committing the biggest folly of your existence and tying your nuptial knot with a marital misfit who you have heretofore only fooled yourself into thinking was your Mr. Right. It's not *unheard* of, okay?

But before you do anything drastic, sit yourself down and ask yourself, from the bottom of your heart, if you and your new love interest could put up with the trials and tribulations that your fiancé and you have already proven you can survive. If there's even a glimmer of doubt, get a grip. Acknowledge that fantasizing was lots of fun (well-deserved fun, considering the stress load under which you've been bearing up). But then get on with the business of officially turning your betrothed into your life partner.

And a life partner is still what you want—isn't it?

EMERGENCY BAILOUTS

Well, then again, maybe it's not! Maybe you are one of those brides-to-be whose eleventh-hour fantasies turn not so much to substitute husbands but rather to the option of having no husband at all. Maybe your doubts and dreads are at this moment fixating not so much on your chosen mate but on the institution of marriage itself.

You can't pick up a magazine or browse a bookstore without running smack up against an article or book about the grim statistics on *un*successful marriage. And chances are you personally know some people whose optimistic attempts at wedlock have ended in collapse. So, hey (a fevered part of your stressed-out brain may counsel at this Last-Minute-itis juncture), *why try at all?* You can still opt for a different, less conventional lifestyle.

There's still time to bail out, says your wedding "spoiler" voice. If you could stop being so lily-livered and summon up the courage to call it off, send the relatives back home *sans* shrimp puffs, and swear off this silly marriage idea once and for all, what would you do then? Why, lots of things! You could:

• *Enter a Convent*—Vespers, vows of silence, candlelight vigils, . . . maybe even chastity belts! Consider the peace and quiet that can be yours when you opt for a stint behind stone walls, far from worldly temptations. You won't need much of a wardrobe, and there's always the outside chance of sainthood being bestowed upon you.

• *Become a Cave Yogi*—Meditation, fasting, levitation . . . Nirvana! Consider the advantages of being one with the universe as opposed to merely being one with your fiancé. Disciples will come from miles around to leave food and flowers at your cave entrance. You need only crawl out and collect once they've gone away. There's a lot to be said for the bliss of utter solitude. You'll never again have to suffer on one of those days when your hair just won't cooperate.

• *Start Your Own Biosphere Project*—Flora, fauna, the perfect ecosystem! Gather a few scientifically-minded friends (preferably women friends, possibly some guys you'll *never* be tempted to marry!) and build yourself a hermetically sealed dome stocked with exactly the right mix of life-forms. A well-written grant proposal can earn you millions in taxpayer dollars as you proceed with your experiment in toxin-free (and husband-free) living.

• *Head Off on a Quest*—The Holy Grail, the Grand Unification Theory, cold fusion, the perfect little black dress, a truly delicious fat-free chocolate chip cookie . . . Decide what it is you want to find and pledge never to rest until you have found it. There's no time for marriage in this obsessive scenario. Keep at it with vigor and you will be a moving target for the rest of your life.

• *Start a Rock Band*—Black-leather jumpsuits, slide guitars, MTV videos! Be footloose and fancy-free and tour America's concert halls and stadiums. If you get lonely, there will be roadies . . . and groupies. No moss grows on a rock-and-roll mama.

• *Join the Peace Corps*—Jungles, mountain villages, developing nations. There is no shortage of places where assistance is needed—and, really, won't you feel much better about yourself if you pack your bags tonight and go offer it than if you stick around for Cousin Wayne's reprise of "Feelings" and then head off on some hedonistic honeymoon?

• *Run for Political Office*—Kiss babies, write position papers, hit the campaign trail! It's certainly time-consuming enough to keep your mind off your jilted beau. And having a spouse is only a hindrance in political life—because then the press gets to look for skeletons in *two* closets instead of one.

• *Man an Earth-Orbiting Space Station*—Comets, constellations, cosmic majesty. Sample the glory of the firmament up close and personal. So what if NASA says you'll need some *training* or that you have to meet some silly *requirements*. You're a go-getter, aren't you? So, go where no bride-to-be has ever gone before. Aside from the fact that your groom is unlikely to track you down, here's the best part: *weightlessness*.

All right, so your spoiler voice has had its say. And though some of its suggested alternatives may seem appalling, you might just have to admit that, given your current state of mind, a few sound rather appealing. But, as you ready yourself for that long procession to the altar, you might just as well come to terms, once and for all, with the fact that no lifestyle you can choose is apt to offer you a panacea.

Is marriage an *ideal* arrangement? Certainly not. It was fraught with complexities even at its inception, when men and women married for strictly practical (i.e., financial and social) rather than emotional reasons. It's even more complicated now that we expect so much from it on every level, wanting our spouses to be helpmates, lovers, best pals, confidantes, corporate partners, and devoted parents to our children. But if there is a better way for the majority of us to bumble along through life, it has yet to be discovered or invented.

Bumble ahead, then. You mustn't feel guilty for your Last-Minute-itis and your last-chance fantasies. Just understand what lies behind them.

> FEAR: "I keep wondering if I'm doing the right thing. I have an urge to take up with a new boyfriend or maybe even disappear without a trace. I feel so

trapped. Why do they call it wed*lock*? *I've got to get out of here!*"

FALLACY: You're having difficulty reconciling your last-minute doubts with your lifelong desire to marry. You'd always heard that grooms had such doubts, but *brides*? Come on. After all, you've been dreaming about your wedding since you were four. So, if you're scared, you think (a) it's wrong to feel that way; and (b) if you do have that feeling, you should do something about it—like run!

REALITY: First of all, no *feeling* is ever wrong. And certainly not this one. Last-Minute-itis and last-chance fantasies are the most normal thing in the world, regardless of your gender, regardless of how much you love your partner, and irrespective of how much you truly want to get married. Secondly, just because you have a feeling doesn't mean you have to take action on it.

REMEDY: Now is a good time to learn, if you haven't already, that you can be the master of your emotions—not their servant. Have your fears, have your fantasies. They're all part of the glorious warp and woof of the mystery we call the mind. Now take a deep breath and get married anyhow!

CHAPTER NINE

I DO, ALREADY!

Love does not consist in gazing at each other, but in looking together in the same direction.

—ANTOINE DE SAINT-EXUPÉRY

Incredibly enough, after all the buildup, all the anticipation, all the fun, and all the aggravation, your engagement period is about to draw to its natural conclusion. And today is the day.

The second you awaken in the morning, you feel somehow different, already transformed, though you can't put your finger on how or why. You draw your first few semiconscious breaths, notice a flutter in your stomach, focus, for a moment, on your heart beating just a smidgen harder and faster than usual.

For a nanosecond or so you wonder, What's going on? Then the realization hits you. Ah! (Can it be?) This is your last morning as a single woman.

Wow. Part of you may feel the urge to languish under the covers for a while, savoring the awesome sense of change that's in the air. Part of you may look around for a stuffed animal to cling to, as you nostalgically recall the time when you were a little girl and weddings meant only a chance to dress up, enjoy a "grown-up" dance standing atop Daddy's feet, and come home with a lace-encased cluster of candied almonds to sample.

But part of you is ready to spring out of bed like a roaring dynamo. For there is a great deal to which you must attend. And not a moment to lose!

According to the standard bridal-guide checklists, you'll need to reconfirm your transportation arrangements (keep an ear out for those unexpected traffic snafus), double-check on bouquets and boutonnieres, find and bring (*where* did you put it?) the marriage license, and pack yourself an emergency duffel that allows for virtually all contingencies (don't forget the extra panty hose, makeup, scissors, safety pins, needle and thread, and spot remover).

But according to human nature, you'll probably forget *something*. Wedding lore is replete with stories of brides who showed up at their wedding site at the appointed hour without their bouquets, without their veils, without their Purple Haze eyeshadow and Moulin Rouge blusher, and even without what most would consider a critical piece of feminine underclothing. It's also full of stories of brides who showed up late because they didn't happen to hear that their route to the church or synagogue coincided with the path of a presidential motorcade or a Save the Whales demonstration.

You'll probably be better off if, right up front, you add to your checklist the task of overlooking something—since it's only acknowledging the inevitable. In the end such minicatastrophes have a way of working out. It's amazing what wizards of improvisation brides become when their husbands-to-be and all their guests await.

Once your minor glitches have been dealt with, you will realize that they were never really that important. Of far greater import are the wedding customs and rituals that come once everyone and everything's in place.

Soon you will be taking your vows, promising to stand by each other, no matter what twists of fate come along. You'll be exchanging rings, whose circular shapes have denoted the concept of infinity since humankind began conveying ideas through symbols. Then, when leaving your ceremony, you'll be pelted with rice by friends and relations, a tradition that signifies wishes for a newlywed couple's abundance—and fertility.

Later, at the reception, your groom will dance with your mother and you with his father, to signify the merging of two clans. You and your husband (yes, *husband*) will feed each other slices of cake, a custom that displays how you plan to nurture each other. The best man will toast your future, and you'll toss your flowers to a future bride. At last, you and the love of your life will head out the door and toward your honeymoon, that idyllic holiday that marks the transition from single to married life—and from Pre-Marital Syndrome to (you guessed it!) Post-Marital Syndrome.

Your week in Aruba, fortnight in France, or what have you will be wonderful. And goodness knows you both deserve a rest after all you've been through. But, as everyone knows, a honeymoon offers, even more than most vacations, a respite from reality.

Samuel Johnson's dictionary describes the honeymoon as a period of marriage when "there is nothing but tenderness and pleasure." But after that it's back to daily life and "for real" marriage, where, though tenderness and pleasure ought certainly to play a part, they do not form the entire picture.

If you're like most of us, you'll find that marriage requires some getting used to. This book began by discussing the plethora of expectations every prospective bride and groom brings to their marriage. To some extent, everyone's expectations are different. But in this day and age, more than at any other time in the history of our species, virtually every newlywed's expectations have one thing in common: They are very, very high.

As family therapist W. Robert Beavers has commented, "markedly increased expectations for marriage have not been accompanied by the increased skills necessary to fulfill such expectations."[1] Incredibly enough, some of the most commonsense "people skills" and thoughtful attitudes that intelligent people employ in their professional dealings and some of the common courtesies they exhibit in relationship with their friends and colleagues seem to fall by the wayside when it comes to domestic dealings.

With a spouse, the very person to whom they were so successful at showing their best side during courtship, people often show their worst side on a fairly consistent basis. Naturally the marriage suffers when neither party makes an effort to consciously hold himself or herself up to mature standards.

In many cases it simply never occurred to *either* party that there are some fundamental steps that they can take to foster a more loving and fulfilling, and infinitely less stressful, marriage. If you are one of the many, many newlyweds who thinks that marriage is simply supposed to "turn out right," as if by hocus-pocus, think again.

Like your engagement period, marriage can benefit mightily from your dedicated best efforts—including, of course, your tolerance, your flexibility, and your willingness to listen with an open mind and an open heart. But let's get specific.

As a wedding gift to you, what follows are ten rules of thumb for getting your marriage off on a positive path and keeping it there for all time. If you don't get a chance to read them on your honeymoon, that's understandable. But don't let too much time elapse upon your homecoming before you study them and put them into practice. For they are what will help you get where you're heading.

FROM ENGAGEMENT TO ETERNITY

BEFORE YOU TRY TO CHANGE YOUR SPOUSE, TRY CHANGING YOUR RESPONSE TO YOUR SPOUSE

I once worked with a woman named Sue, who was terribly annoyed by her husband's snoring, which was in fact quite loud due to a deviated septum in his nose. She contended that his racket kept her up nights and that she was becoming seriously sleep-deprived. Her husband, who was very considerate and truly did not want to disturb her, felt badly that there was nothing he could do about the situation.

He suggested she use earplugs or a white-noise machine to muffle the sound. But the wife ruled these out. She said earplugs would probably be uncomfortable and white-noise machines were just a silly gimmick she was sure wouldn't work. Still, the snoring did not stop, and Sue became crankier and crankier over the situation until one day she said, "You have simply got to fix this, I don't care how!"

Her husband consulted his doctor and decided to have an operation on his deviated septum, even though this would involve some physical discomfort and several missed days of work. The wife was delighted, because she anticipated the problem would be solved once and for all—and because all her friends remarked how much her husband must love her to undergo surgery for her benefit. "What a guy I married," she thought!

So, the operation took place, and as predicted, Sue's husband snored no more. Instead, though, he produced an even louder nocturnal cacophony, which sounded, Sue said, like a pile of leaves rustling in the wind, followed by a shrill clenched-teeth whistle.

Eventually Sue purchased earplugs and a white-noise machine after all. They do help, she contends, though that darned whistle sometimes wakes her up anyhow. "I guess," she says, "I should have tried to adjust in the first place."

Though this story seems rather humorous, its moral cannot be too strongly stressed. Truer words were never spoken than, "I should have tried to adjust in the first place."

As you embark upon your marriage, you will discover numerous behaviors of your spouse that you will no doubt want him to change. Before you start making any such demands, try altering your reaction to that behavior instead.

You may find that with a little creativity you can find a way to acclimate to the behavior, or that with a little good humor and forbearance you can overlook it. With time you may simply forget about it or—who knows—even grow to feel fond of it.

If you make demands upon your spouse to change, beware—for they may backfire. While it's okay to set limits and state preferences, being demanding can get your partner's defenses up and make him intractable. Even if your spouse *does* agree he wants to change whatever particular behavior is causing you grief, be aware of two caveats.

Many kinds of changes (quitting smoking for example, or losing weight or cutting back on impulsive spending) do not tend to "stick" unless the person undergoing the change *does so for himself.* Other kinds of changes (e.g., Sue's husband's surgical snoring cure) may, of course, "stick"—even if they are undertaken solely for the benefit of one's mate. But as we've seen, you may find, after all, that the solution sometimes turns out to be more annoying than the original problem.

REMEMBER THE POLARIZATION PRINCIPLE—AND MOVE IN YOUR PARTNER'S DIRECTION

After marriage Stephanie and Ted rapidly discovered that they had different ways of approaching impending deadlines. If someone's birthday was coming up, for example, Stephanie tended to buy a card and gift weeks ahead of time. Ted's style was to stop on the way to the birthday party and purchase what was needed. Stephanie grew very unnerved by what she called Ted's waiting games. She feared something "would slip through a crack." Her automatic response was to start taking total charge of matters that would affect them both.

So if the car had to be inspected, Stephanie would tend to it a month before the sticker-expiration date. If taxes were due, she would have them prepared with April 15 far off on the horizon. Sooner or later (usually quite a bit later—but, never too late as to be really neglectful), Ted would in fact make up his mind to tackle those same chores. But when he broached the subjects with his overcompensating wife, he would find everything had been efficiently handled.

You don't need to be a rocket scientist to guess what happened over time. As Stephanie grew more and more hyperresponsible, Ted grew more and more nonchalant. In the back of his mind he always knew that while he perhaps ought to be tending to this-and-that, Stephanie would take care of it—in fact she probably already had.

When Stephanie came to see me in my office, she was distraught over an impending move to a new apartment that she and her husband were about to undertake. She said, "There is so much to do, and I know if I leave it to Ted, he won't get it done, so I have to do it all!" Then she enumerated a list of tasks long enough to keep her busy round the clock for thirty days to come.

"Won't he deal with any of that?" I asked her. She said he would not. She explained about their divergence in styles and then proudly told me how she had come routinely to "forestall disaster" in their lives by taking matters into her own capable hands. The only drawback, she complained, was "the more I handle everything, the less he handles anything."

Bingo. I pointed out to her that she had only to reverse this process for the dynamics to shift.

On my advice Stephanie went home and did nothing

regarding the move. She neither packed boxes, nor sent out change of address cards, nor called for movers' estimates—all items that had been on the original list she'd rattled off to me.

A week went by, then two. It took a lot of strength for Stephanie to resist her urge to dive in and do it all, but—to her credit—she bravely managed to do nothing. Finally Ted noticed that no moving cartons were piling up in the hallway as he'd anticipated. He checked the date on the calendar and casually mentioned to Stephanie that moving day was drawing near. She smiled and said, "Oh, not to worry. There's plenty of time." When she was still saying the same thing a week later, Ted actually brought home some cartons and began packing them himself. One night he stayed up well past midnight sending out change-of-address cards. The next day he said, "Hey, Steph, could you help me out a little here?" And she did help out—but she did not rush in and take over.

Together Stephanie and Ted managed their move as a twosome. And Stephanie learned a valuable lesson.

Whether you tend to start off a marriage with similar or dissimilar attitudes, a very common marital dynamic is *polarization*. In Chapter 4 you learned how couples are prone to polarize over issues of money. As the above story shows, polarization can take place around *all kinds* of issues, not just financial ones.

Whenever two people join together in an intimate situation, they tend to act out opposite sides of any given human impulse. Should you notice this happening in your marriage, don't insist that your spouse do it your way (that probably won't be effective anyhow). Instead, change your course 180 degrees and do it *his* way.

Then watch what happens.

Marriage seeks a natural balance, and in most cases you will find that as you go your husband's way, he'll move your way. With a little patience you could find yourself meeting in the middle for a happy rendezvous.

COMPLETE HONESTY IS FOR SADISTS AND MASOCHISTS—LEARN HOW, WHY, AND WHEN TO EDIT YOURSELF

When Roger and Karen got married, they vowed to each other to be totally open and honest all of the time. And they both took this promise literally. If Karen bought a new outfit and Roger didn't like it, he said so. Never mind that she had already told him that (a) she adored it; and (b) it was purchased on sale and was nonreturnable.

Likewise, if Roger asked his wife a leading question like "Even though you act nice to my mother, you really can't stand her, right?" Karen would be apt to reply. "You know, you're right. I really think she's obnoxious."

You probably won't be surprised to learn that before long this husband and wife were having a huge number of high-decibel arguments. But perhaps the biggest and loudest quarrel arose when Karen and Roger went to the beach one day and Karen noticed her husband eyeing a remarkably gorgeous woman with what Karen herself considered the "body of a Greek goddess." She turned to him and asked, "Tell me the truth now. You're having a sexual fantasy about her, aren't you?" After he replied in the affirmative, it was not long before he—not to mention every sunbather within a half mile or so—realized this was definitely *not* what she'd wanted to hear.

Although in the abstract one might deem honesty the best policy in marriage, the reality of it is that complete truth telling at all times is not just impractical, it's unkind.

Learning how and when to discreetly edit oneself is all part of being a grown-up. It's called having tact. You do it at work. You do it with your friends. Please be considerate enough to do it with your spouse.

Perhaps you don't like telling out-and-out untruths. But be aware that there are many shade-of-gray options between the two extremes.

If you don't like the way your partner looks in a particular piece of clothing, you can say, "I like you even better in the blue, honey. It really sets off your eyes. Why don't you wear that tonight." If you have recurrent fantasies of your mother-in-law staked to an anthill in the desert sun, for goodness' sake, don't mention it—even if prodded by your mate. And if you harbor pleasant postmarital sexual fantasies about someone other than your spouse, keep them to yourself. Although this is a perfectly normal and extremely common aspect of human behavior, it is one that is best savored in the inviolate privacy of one's own psyche (as are a good number of our thoughts).

So much has been written about "sharing one's feelings" in marriage that it's no wonder couples often get the erroneous idea that there are no limits on this dictum that might be beneficial. But think of it this way: Suppose you went through one entire week—or even just one day—uttering nothing but the truth, the whole truth, to everyone. Frightening, isn't it? You could, very easily, lose your job and your best friend. Someone might punch you in the nose, or worse.

It's unreasonable to expect your spouse to take all your unexpurgated truths in stride. And it's a giant cop-out for you to say, "Hey, you can't blame me. I'm just being open."

LEARN FROM EXPERIENCE TO STEER CLEAR OF "HOT SPOTS"

For the most part Debbie thought of her husband, Charlie, as an even-tempered fellow. Though, like all married couples, they had disagreements from time to time, for the most part theirs were mild. *Except* when they revolved around Charlie's older brother, Elliott.

Elliott was a man who seemed to have it all. A highly regarded physician, he was the author of several well-known books and the winner of countless humanitarian awards. He owned a lovely house in Marin County, California, and an apartment in San Francisco overlooking the bay. He had always been the apple of his parents' eye—and a thorn in his younger brother's side.

When Charlie and Debbie got married, Elliott came to the

wedding and proceeded to charm the bride's entire family. He presented the newlywed couple with a full set of Richard Ginori china he had purchased for them in Rome. Inevitably Debbie, who had not heard much about Elliott previously, had only the nicest impression of him. Not long after the wedding she mentioned to her husband how much her parents liked his brother and even suggested trying to fix him up with one of her cousins who also lived in the Bay Area. To her surprise her mild-mannered husband launched into a tirade about his brother's unsuitability to marry her cousin or anyone else. "He's a workaholic and an egomaniac," Charlie said. "I can't believe you were snowed by him. You probably wish you'd married him instead, huh?"

Debbie decided to drop the matter for the time being, rationalizing that Charlie was just having a bad day. But she found herself once again singing Elliott's praises when she happened to catch him being interviewed about his latest book on a national morning talk show. "Guess who was on TV today, sounding absolutely brilliant?" she asked her husband when he walked through the door that evening. Before long Charlie was ranting and raving about how this kind of attention would make his brother even more insufferable. And before much longer one of the Richard Ginori plates was lying in pieces in the kitchen sink, having "slipped" out of Charlie's hand.

You'd think that Debbie would be getting the picture by now that there was simply nothing to be gained from saying favorable things about Elliott and that perhaps she might steer clear of the subject of her brother-in-law altogether. But being a peacemaker by nature, she determined, instead, to see what she could do to bring Charlie and Elliott closer together. To this end she kept trying to convince her husband that his brother was really a "good guy." But this was the last thing Charlie wanted to hear, and every attempt she made at mending the rift between brothers led to a rift between husband and wife.

Here is a situation where someone is acting out of the best of intentions, but causing damage nonetheless. Though Debbie was convinced she was on high moral ground, trying to mitigate her husband's resentment of his sibling, she made a critical mistake in judgment. She remained single-minded in pursuing her idealistic agenda, while remaining oblivious to the fact that, by doing so, she was trouncing on her husband's emotional Achilles heel. Instead of letting her own experience guide her, she relied on an abstract notion of what was "right." And that was wrong.

From the day we emerge from the womb into this world, much of the way we learn and adapt to our physical and emotional environment is through trial and error. We try something out, get rewarded in some way, or achieve a goal we wanted to achieve, and so we do it again. We try something else out and end up falling on our butts, literally or figuratively. Before long we may give up that unsuccessful behavior.

To a great extent, engaging in trial and error is also the way we will adapt to marriage. No matter how much advice you solicit on what makes other people's marriages work, each marriage is, in certain ways, an entity unto itself—a system with its own internal rules and self-regulating mechanisms. Be observant and these dynamics will reveal themselves to you.

Then try to steer clear of your partner's irrational "hot spots." You may find your largely reasonable mate to be absolutely irrational when it comes to one or two areas. When you think about it, who isn't? If these are areas that can be side-stepped without causing undue harm to the relationship, go ahead and sidestep them. Whatever you do, don't dwell on them.

No matter how bizarre you may deem your partner's reaction—or overreaction—pro or con, to a given subject (his brother, say, or Republicans, or the queen of England, or Santa Claus), don't bait him by trying to get him to abandon his stance. Such habits die hard, and who are you to say they should die at all.

WHEN IT COMES TO A HAPPY MARRIAGE, PRAISE AND PLAY PAVE THE WAY

I once met a couple at a party who, when they learned I counseled couples, told me that they would never require such a service. They felt confident that they had worked out the formula for an ideal marriage, which was to hold a monthly "summit" between the two of them where all their grievances could be aired. If one partner felt the other had been neglectful, in some area, they said so. If one felt they had too much responsibility and the other not enough, that was said also. Complaints were aired about everything from money to housework to sex.

This couple—let's call them Mr. and Mrs. Smith—said they were more conscious about working at their marriage than some people, even though things might look otherwise on the surface. As they said the words *some people,* they pointedly glanced in the direction of our hosts, a couple who were openly giggly and playful with each other, who both flattered and teased each other frequently, and who often addressed each other by what the Smiths called "silly" pet names. The Smiths clearly thought our hosts did not see marriage as an "enterprise" the way they said they did.

I never saw nor heard from this serious-minded couple again, but about two years later our mutual friends who had given the party mentioned that the Smiths were getting a divorce. Somehow, they said, they weren't surprised to hear it. It never seemed to them, they said, like Mr. and Mrs. Smith were very supportive of each other, nor that they were having any *fun* being married.

Apparently Mr. and Mrs. Smith held the idea that marriage was serious business, and no laughing matter. They were both correct and incorrect. It is serious business, but heaven help the husbands and wives for whom it is not a laughing matter too.

Where the Smiths went wrong is that while they were

diligent about sharing their complaints, they never seemed to share praise with each other. They never made room for the spontaneous cheerleading and the good-natured goofiness that are the daily bread and butter of a sound marriage. So concerned were they with ferreting out potential problems that they could not see the forest for the trees. The *biggest* problem they had was that they never focused on the positive, and they simply never lightened up!

As often as possible, say something kind and complimentary to your partner. Without such positive reinforcement none of us would have thrived as children. As adults we still need such communications in order to flourish and function as our best selves.

Another thing we never would have thrived without was affectionate play from our caregivers. In marriage, too, the role of play must not be underestimated. It's not only good for the soul but good for working through practical matters. Studies have shown that using play and humor in marriage helps partners let down their usual defenses, explore sensitive issues, and give healthy vent to aggression.[2] Ironically the very "diversions" that the Smiths thought were so frivolous offered better inroads for coping with marital sore spots than routine face-offs of debate and complaint.

DON'T MAKE YOUR SPOUSE YOUR WHOLE WORLD

When Caitlin and Paul got married, they were very, very happy to be able to see so much of each other. The two had lived in different cities during most of their courtship, commuting between Philadelphia and Chicago. It was only shortly before the wedding that Paul got the transfer he had been seeking and was finally able to move to Chicago.

For these newlywed lovebirds, just sharing the simple chores of daily life seemed like Paradise. They got excited about shopping and cooking together, even about doing the laundry! For months and months they both raced straight home from work to each other's arms every night. And since they swore they preferred each other's company to anyone else's, they limited their weekend social engagements dramatically. Unless a pressing commitment demanded their presence, Paul and Caitlin tended to stay home together or dine out at a cozy neighborhood restaurant, claiming their favorite table for two.

Sometimes they'd undertake some activity together, such as jogging and bike riding, which they both enjoyed. But each tended to let many of the activities they routinely engaged in before marriage slide, especially if these were pastimes for which the other had little affinity. Caitlin, for example, never seemed to go swimming at the Y anymore, and she lost touch with the crowd she used to swim with. Paul never took the time to seek out a new group of bridge players, as he'd said he would do before he moved to his new city. Even though bridge was a passion of his, he knew his wife had no patience for it, and he hated the thought of spending a night each week doing something that didn't include her.

Besides not making many new friends in Chicago, Paul found himself falling out of touch with those he'd left behind in Philadelphia. The calls from old buddies grew fewer and farther between. But for a long time Paul didn't seem to notice, or mind—any more than Caitlin minded slipping away from many of the friends she'd had for years.

Just after their first anniversary Paul found he had to go back to Philadelphia for a two-week conference and training seminar at his company headquarters. Caitlin couldn't accompany him, so they spent the two weeks apart. During that time Caitlin noticed how difficult it was to make any dinner dates with her friends, most of whom had resigned themselves to the fact that she was no longer available and who had closed up the resultant gaps in their social schedules. She did go swimming at the Y, but found herself so out of practice that she was nearly breathless after a few laps.

As for Paul, his old friends in Philadelphia said they were glad when he rang them up, but even those who found time to see him seemed somehow distant. It was as if things had changed, Paul thought. And of course they had changed. He hadn't even been aware that one of his closest pals had gotten engaged and that another had become a father.

When Paul returned home, he seemed restless. Before long he and Caitlin were growing irritable with each other for no reason either of them could put their finger on. They still spent almost all their free time together, but began to notice they weren't enjoying it as much as they used to. There didn't seem to be as much to say. There weren't many different experiences or observations to compare. Each of them secretly wondered what had gone wrong—after all, they'd been so blissfully cocooned for so long. Why did things seem to be going sour?

The honeymoon period tends to include a certain amount of natural "nesting" behavior as husbands and wives settle in for the long run, and more than a few couples tend to be somewhat reclusive in their earliest phase of marriage. Such seclusion can be very satisfying for a while. Indeed it evokes the same sense of psychic completion that a mother and a newborn experience as they cling to each other, largely oblivious to external events. But there is little advantage in stretching this time past its natural limits, as Paul and Caitlin did. Just because you are married is no reason to isolate permanently.

So, newlyweds, *get a life* and live it to its fullest.

If that means spending time at something you enjoy but that your spouse is not wild about, so be it. If that includes picking up the phone and contacting the friends with whom you've lost touch, do it (and don't be embarrassed to tell them you're sorry).

There's no arguing that a solid, loving marriage is a wonderful thing. But if you want to keep the relationship on firm footing, don't forget that the world is full of wonderful things and wonderful people. If you go off and experience some of it without your spouse's company, and he without yours, that is all the more you will have to talk about and laugh about and empathize with later on. If the two of you have the chance to spend time together in the company of people whom you care about and who care about you, that's a lot of healthy stimulation for the bond between you as husband and wife.

DON'T BOTH GO CRAZY AT THE SAME TIME

One night, not too long into his marriage, Brad came home in a rage. It seems his boss, who often was a source of irritation, had once again infuriated him. "Do you know what that jerk did today?" Brad asked his wife, Tori. "He took credit for that market-research study after I broke my back putting it together. I can't stand it anymore. I'd rather *starve* than work for him. He's not fit to carry my lunch pail. Why, I have a good mind to pick up the phone and call him at home and quit right now. Better yet, maybe I'll go over there and sock him."

Tori's reaction was equally histrionic—but she had another reason for outrage. "What do you *mean,* quit your job," she cried with alarm. "How irresponsible can you be? We've got bills up to our eyeballs. You'd better learn how to swallow your pride, or we'll be in big trouble."

Brad was incensed by her response. And all that anger he'd had toward his boss suddenly found a new target. "Hey, thanks for the support," he said sarcastically. "If that's the way you feel about it, maybe I should just move out."

"If that's the way *you* feel about it," replied his wife, "maybe *I* ought to move out."

On and on the two went until both of them were actually opening dresser drawers and throwing underwear into suitcases, anxious to see who could beat the other out the door to prove their point.

Though they ultimately made up, the memories of this calamitous quarrel lived on in infamy. Today Tori says she knows just how easily it could have been avoided by following one simple rule.

Where Tori went wrong was in adding fuel to her husband's fire. Brad came home in an ornery mood, but instead of trying to calm him down, his wife got him battling with *her*. Certainly it seemed like Brad was being irrational with all his talk of quitting his job on the spur of the moment or punching out his boss. But everybody has a tendency to talk and think irrationally sometimes. In a marriage, however, only one person at a time should be allowed to go off the deep end.

In fairness, this is sometimes easier said than done. In marriage, feelings can travel between partners with the speed and intensity of an electric current. It's so easy to get "zapped" with a high-voltage dose of hysteria and anger. But acting on those induced feelings is a mistake. In fact, in the face of a spouse's ranting and raving, one needs to muster as much self-control as possible and remain calm.

Tori would have been better off echoing Brad's sentiments that he was being mistreated at work while keeping her own fears of insolvency in check. Certainly she had a right to be frightened about her husband up and quitting his job if their financial situation was precarious, but once Brad felt validated—and appreciated by someone other than his boss—chances are his desire to behave precipitously would have been tempered.

So try to make a verbal agreement with your spouse right up front that you both won't "go crazy" simultaneously. Enforcing such a bargain is really acting out of enlightened self-interest. It will keep your fights from escalating to a point where both of you say and do things you will later regret. It will help keep balance and perspective in the household. Most of all, it will give you your chance to "go crazy" too—without having to endure cataclysmic marital consequences.

DON'T TRY TO SOLVE ALL YOUR PROBLEMS AT ONCE

When Bill and Christine first got married, they faced a housing dilemma. Before marriage each had a small rent-stabilized apartment in New York City, which they were renting for considerably less than market value. In other words their places were both real deals—a commodity that no one wants to relinquish. For them to have given up both cheap apartments and rented a new place that could have comfortably accommodated both of them and their belongings was, at the time, simply undoable. So they decided to live together in Christine's apartment and keep Bill's apartment for storage space. But this turned out not to be terribly convenient—sort of "like having your closet across town," as they put it.

With some careful budgeting and a loan from their parents, though, they were, after a year or so, able to put together enough for a down payment on a condominium where they would at last have ample space. Bill was very happy and wanted to go ahead and buy the place immediately.

But Christine was anxious. She told Bill that while the condo was roomy for now, what about five years or so from now when they had children? He replied, "Well, we can sell it." Christine wasn't calmed, though. She started obsessing on what would happen if the real estate market took another dive and they *couldn't* sell it. Where would their children sleep then?

Bill said, "Well, we'll cross that bridge when we come to it. Besides, no one ever knows for sure whether they can even have children until they try."

Now his wife was really anxious. She stewed for a day or two, then said, "You know, I think it would be a good idea if we went for fertility tests." Bill said he thought that was really jumping the gun, and when Christine called her doctor, *she* said, "Just try to relax, best thing for you both."

That having been settled for the time being, Bill thought they could go ahead with their plans to buy the condo. But no. Christine still seemed reluctant to go forward. Now she was worried about what would happen if one of their parents died and the other was widowed. "It could happen very suddenly. They might want to move in with us—at least for a while. Where on earth would we put them?"

Now Bill got anxious. He had simply never imagined one of his parents or one of his wife's parents moving in with them. He did not necessarily relish the thought and said so, which led Christine to criticize his "selfishness." Which led to another of the couple's many conflicts about hypothetical situations that might or might never occur.

Over the course of one's married life, many problems are bound to present themselves, and many transitions will unfold—each with its own set of challenges. Like Christine and Bill, you and your spouse will move to new homes, deal with having (or not having) kids, and contend with the aging of your parents, among other things.

There is simply no anticipating what adaptations each new set of circumstances will require on your part. And if you try to figure it out ahead of time, the only thing that's certain is that you will drive yourself, and your partner, to distraction. What's more, like Christine, you may feel paralyzed, unable to take any action to solve your immediate problems, because you are so distracted by any possible negative future consequences of the things you do today.

Having been presented with the opportunity to solve her and her husband's frustrating housing arrangements was a blessing. But rather than seeing it as such, Christine saw it as a domino in a series of new frustrations. In her obsessive quest to unearth and presolve all potential future snags *ad infinitum,* she was depriving herself and her spouse of the pleasures of enjoying the moment. She was also placing tremendous and needless pressure on them both.

Why would she do this? Perhaps she was one of the many people who mistakenly equate getting married with coming to the end of a story and living "happily ever after." (It's a common misconception, for this is, after all, the way all the *fairy tales* concluded.) But marriage is not an ending, of course, it is a beginning. Now you have a helpmate beside you to help you meet life's hurdles. But you have not been granted immunity from those hurdles by virtue of your marriage license.

Just rise to meet them, one by one, as they come along, and you'll be amazed at how resourceful you both can be.

KNOW THINGS SOMETIMES GET WORSE BEFORE THEY GET BETTER

After Shelley and Rick got married, Shelley started becoming very annoyed and angry at her husband because of what she considered his excessive bent for order. She hated the fact that he was fastidious about everything from his personal appearance to the way the magazines were stacked on the coffee table. She especially resented that he straightened up after her all the time, hanging up the coat she'd left on the living room sofa, picking up the glasses she drank from, and so on. And even though Rick never criticized her for being messy, she said she could just *feel* him judging her.

Sometimes she would look in her husband's closet and see all his shirts and ties and shoes in their neat little rows and Shelley would just grit her teeth. "What an uptight, rigid, controlling guy I married," she'd think. "What did I get myself into? Now I'm trapped!"

The funny thing was that if you had asked Shelley before her wedding what she thought about her husband's penchant for neatness, she probably would have said, "Oh, I think it's kind of cute."

In every marriage there comes a time when, both literally and metaphorically, the honeymoon is over. Then there begins a phase that many newlyweds find unsettling. Let's call it the "What Have I Done?" phase.

In her "What Have I Done?" phase, Shelley experienced a very common phenomenon. She zeroed in on a trait she'd found endearing before the wedding and found it torturous now that she was "stuck" with it for the rest of her life. Like many other newlyweds she did this for two reasons.

First, she was undergoing what's known as a "splitting" process. It's almost inevitable that during the honeymoon one's beloved seems wholly wonderful (as wonderful, if not more so, than he did when you first met him—i.e., before the trials of Pre-Marital Syndrome set in). But after that we experience a psychic counterforce that catapults our thoughts in the other direction.

You probably remember from physics that every action has an equal and opposite reaction, and that's what's emotionally operative here. What was formerly a too-good-to-be-true scenario now seems a too-bad-to-be-true one. Of course, neither case is the reality. What Shelley has is a neat husband whose behavior is sometimes frustrating. He is neither saint nor sinner, but a human being with a particular set of habits— none of them deliberately crafted to make her miserable.

What turned out to exacerbate Shelley's reaction, however, was another common psychic phenomenon. As it turned out, deep down Shelley was somewhat confused as to just *which* human being she was dealing with. In our talks in couples' counseling she realized that it was her *mother's* neatness that had long been a source of frustration to her, and to some degree she was reexperiencing the rage she felt when her very controlling mother lambasted her for being "sloppy."

How very common it is, during marriage's "What Have I Done?" phase for us to mix up the feelings we have toward our spouse with the feelings we harbor toward a parent. Until now our parents were the family we had always known. Now our partner is family, and we unwittingly overlay one situation atop the other.

Shelley, you'll remember, had the feeling that her husband was critical of her own comparatively relaxed housekeeping habits. But in fact he never said anything defamatory to her at all in that regard. Indeed, when she accused him of this in a couples session, he assured her he had no wish to judge her and that his straightening up after her was, for the most part, an automatic, unpremeditated gesture.

Today Rick still picks up after his wife a little more than she is comfortable with. Sometimes she finds it annoying. And he will admit that, on occasion, he does wish she were a little better organized. Sometimes this couple gets into a tiff about such matters, which is, of course, all part of being married. But having survived the "What Have I Done?" phase, Shelley consciously tries to confine her anger to the situation at hand and the person at hand (her husband, that is, not her mother). She also realizes that her husband is neither all-good nor all-bad. She's well aware that he can love her all the time while still aggravating her and disagreeing with her some of the time.

MARRIAGE IS OFTEN A SELF-FULFILLING PROPHECY

Roberta told me she could always predict when she and her husband were going to have a fight. She said that after one of them came home from an out-of-town business trip, they would always argue. She also said they would quarrel whenever they had to make a long drive to visit her sister and brother-in-law upstate. She mentioned several more circumstances that she said would inevitably yield a conflict between them. Her husband, Barry, agreed. "Yes," he said, "whenever these things happen, we have a fight. It's inevitable. I don't think you can help us."

I said I didn't know if I could help them, but I would like to see each of them individually once before deciding. I saw Roberta alone, and she mentioned Barry would be going away on a business trip in a few days. Obviously she was expecting the conclusion of that trip to yield a quarrel. I told her, "I'm going to see your husband tomorrow, before his trip. You are not to worry. Leave it all to me. When he returns, you two will have one of your most romantic evenings ever."

When I saw Barry, I told him much the same thing. "I saw

your wife yesterday. When you come home from your trip, you will have a very romantic evening instead of your usual fight. Don't worry about a thing."

The day after Barry returned from his business trip, he and his wife each called me. They told me they'd just had a terrific intimate evening together. Each of them thanked me profusely for whatever I had "done" to their spouse.

Needless to say, I had not done a thing to Roberta or to Barry, except to plant in their minds the idea that something else was going to happen than what they were used to. Because each of them was now predicting a good evening, that's what happened.

Many couples therapists use versions of the "prediction task"[3] in their work. Even when couples' fights take place at random times, it can be helpful. Simply by getting a couple individually to write down at nighttime what type of experience they expect to have with their spouse the following day can have a positive impact. It introduces the idea that things *might* go well, and when such is forecasted, it is often the case.[4]

It may sound simplistic to suggest that you stand a better chance of having a good, loving rapport with your spouse if you think you will, but often the best advice *is* simple. In marriage, as in every other worthwhile endeavor, attitude is all-important. If you start from the premise "Things will go badly," they are more apt to go badly. On the other hand, with the right attitude the path to marital harmony is more accessible than most of us imagine.

So there you have your ten wedding presents. May you use them again and again. Your fear may be that you won't be able to put them all into practice and that instead of consciously shaping a thriving, fulfilling marriage you'll sometimes do exactly the wrong thing. Well, there's no fallacy behind that fear. For, of course, at times you *will* do exactly the wrong thing.

Over the course of your marriage you are going to make unreasonable demands on your spouse, say things you shouldn't, forfeit your sense of humor, nag, complain, and generally be a pain. He will too. But if you remain resolute about putting these ten maxims into practice, despite inevitable occasional slips, your rewards will be many and your regrets will be few.

It's been a long road since that magical moment when you let out a breathless "yes" to the question "Will you marry me?" You've wrestled with all kinds of turmoil. You *already* know you're a survivor. And that alone will help you through.

All that's left to say is to wish you a great life together! (And, of course, don't forget to write those thank-you cards, return those extra blenders and ice buckets for store credit, preserve your wedding dress in a garment bag, and get ready to see the friend who caught your bouquet through her bout of Pre-Marital Syndrome.)

NOTES

CHAPTER 4

1. *The Better Homes and Gardens Bride's Book* (Des Moines, Ia.: Special Interest Publications, 1992).

CHAPTER 5

1. Robert J. Sternberg, "Explorations of Love," in *Perspectives in Interpersonal Behavior and Relationships,* edited by D. Perlman and W. Jones (Greenwich, Conn.: JAL Press, 1987).

CHAPTER 6

1. Murray Bowen, *Family Therapy in Clinical Practice* (New York: Jason Aronsen, 1978).

CHAPTER 7

1. Erik Erikson, *Childhood and Society* (New York: W. W. Norton, 1963).

2. Daniel Yankelovich, *New Rules: Searching for Self-Fulfillment in a World Turned Upside Down* (New York: Random House, 1981).

3. Murray Bowen, *Family Therapy in Clinical Practice* (New York: Jason Aronsen, 1978).

4. Una Stannard, *Married Women v. Husbands' Names* (San Francisco: Germainbooks, 1973).

CHAPTER 8

1. Dorothy Tennov, *Love and Limerence* (New York: Stein & Day, 1979).

2. Johan Verhulst, M.D., M.A. "Limerence: Notes on the Nature and Function of Passionate Love," *Psychoanalysis and Contemporary Thought* 7:1 (1984): 115–38.

CHAPTER 9

1. W. Robert Beavers, *Successful Marriage: A Family Systems Approach to Couples Therapy* (New York: W. W. Norton & Company, 1985).

2. William Betcher, *Intimate Play: Creating Romance in Everyday Life* (New York: Viking Penguin, 1987).

3. S. de Shazer, *Patterns of Brief Family Therapy* (New York: Guilford, 1982).

4. Michele Weiner-Davis, *Divorce Busting* (New York: Summit, 1992).

ABOUT THE AUTHOR

Arlene Modica Matthews is the author of *Why Did I Marry You Anyway?*, *Your Money, Your Self,* and coauthor of *How to Manage Your Mother.* She is a psychotherapist in private practice in New York City.